So Much I Want to Tell You

So Much
I Want to
Tell You

LETTERS TO MY LITTLE SISTER

Anna Akana

BALLANTINE BOOKS

NEW YORK

A Ballantine Books Trade Paperback Original

Copyright © 2017 by Anna Akana

Published in the United States by Ballantine Books,
an imprint of Random House, a division of
Penguin Random House LLC, New York.

BALLANTINE and the HOUSE colophon are
registered trademarks of Penguin Random House LLC.

ISBN 978-0-399-59493-9
Ebook ISBN 978-0-399-59492-2

Printed in the United States of America on acid-free paper

randomhousebooks.com

246897531

Book design by Barbara M. Bachman

FOR MY MOTHER, FATHER, AND BROTHER—
WE'VE BEEN TO HELL AND CAME BACK STRONGER.

CONTENTS

—

CONTENTS

Introduction

———

**OUR LIFE IS MADE BY
THE DEATH OF OTHERS.**

—*Leonardo da Vinci*

A lot has happened since my sister killed herself.

She was thirteen years old when she died in 2007. If she were still alive, she'd be in her twenties. She'd be old enough to drink, drive, get married, have kids. I sometimes can't believe she's gone. It feels like she was this person I knew who just disappeared. Kinda like in a romantic relationship. You spend every day with a person for years, until one day you break up. Then they're just gone. Your best friend, your roommate, the person you spent a chunk of your life with. Gone.

Why exactly Kristina killed herself will always be a mystery. Was her suicide an impulsive adolescent decision? Or was it something more? In 2007, the suicide epidemic had only just begun to sweep the nation's teen population. She was bullied in school before bullying was taken seriously and, worse, punished for trying to defend herself. When a group of boys threatened to beat her up after school, Kristina did what she was supposed to do— she told her teachers. For whatever reason, her teachers didn't take the threat seriously. They told her it was probably a joke. It wasn't a joke to Kris, though. She brought an airsoft gun to school for protection and was expelled because of it. This caused a lot of trouble for her at home.

Kristina was able to change schools, but she had a hard time adjusting. She didn't get along well with the kids in her new school, although she was usually great at making friends. When she began to fall behind in her classes, she was diagnosed with dyslexia. Instead of considering treatment, my family approached the diagnosis as an obstacle Kristina could overcome with time and didn't offer her much support.

I'd always had my suspicions that Kristina might have suffered from bipolar disorder, or some other mood disorder. People didn't talk about mental health as much as they should have ten years ago. They still don't, in my opinion. But I'll never know. Maybe she was so hurt and alone and scared that she made choices without fully understanding how permanent they were. Maybe she could no longer handle being bullied and misunderstood by her family. Maybe, if she exists somewhere, she regrets her choice. Maybe it's all of it. Everything.

KRISTINA DIED ON VALENTINE'S DAY. I was on a picnic with my boyfriend at our local park when a terrible feeling came over me in a wave. I leapt to my feet, screaming that we needed to leave immediately. Something was wrong. I packed up our picnic and bolted for the car. That's when my brother, Will, called. He told me Kristina had tried to take her own life. At the time he didn't know that she'd succeeded. But I knew. I felt it.

Weeks later I told my mom that, somehow, I'd known something was wrong. Mom was always the one who had a little bit of a third eye. When she was a kid in the Philippines, she'd have dreams of relatives saying goodbye, only to wake up and find out that they'd passed away in the night. She'd see ghostly figures standing on dirt roads, looking lost and confused. But when Kristina died, Mom said she hadn't felt anything. "I was just sitting downstairs knitting," she said, beginning to cry. Later my sister came to my mom in a dream, to say she was sorry.

She appeared in my dreams too, except my dreams were nightmares: Me and Kristina in a bug-infested house, my arms wrapped around her, trying to protect her, but the bugs kept crawling into her eyes anyway. Then I'd see her standing on the edge of a cliff, body distorted, looking back at me before falling off. These images still haunt me, even ten years later.

MY SISTER LEFT A SUICIDE NOTE, but I was never allowed to read it. I've asked Dad about it all these years later and he insists that he lost it in a move. Whether that's true or he's trying to protect me, I don't know. But from what he told me, the note isn't kind.

"I'm sorry I make everyone so miserable" were her final words. She had a special goodbye for her friends and cousin Frank, but nothing for us. Nothing for us because she was furious with us. She'd fought with every member of my family over something trivial, a sleepover she wasn't allowed to attend. She came into my room last, but I turned her away. The last thing I ever said to her was "I hate you."

Her death didn't feel real for many, many days. I woke up the day after she died expecting her to be in her room, only to find Mom in the closet instead. Together, we cried until our heads felt like they'd cracked in half. The sick feeling in our guts only went away after several hours of sleep. Our faces, however, never changed. The blank, empty expressions remained. I had a constant headache from crying.

I AM KRISTINA'S BIG SISTER. I was supposed to protect her. I was supposed to comfort her. So many times I walked by her room and I could have said something. I don't blame myself anymore, but I do know that there were things I could have done differently. Things I could have said. And perhaps if I had, we wouldn't be where we are today.

I wrote her a letter. I said I was sorry, that I loved her, that I hoped she was okay wherever she was. I asked her to visit me in a dream to say goodbye, because I wanted so badly to see her one last time. I burned the letter, because it seemed like the only way to mail it to the afterworld. And then I cried.

———

I WAS DESTROYED BY KRISTINA'S DEATH. My whole family was. For a very long time it felt like we were broken. Like we were trying to shove the sharp, jagged pieces back together again, but they didn't quite fit.

Whenever someone casually mentioned suicide, hyperbolically or colloquially, I would have horrible flashbacks. I would feel a physical pain in my chest. I'd have to excuse myself to calm myself down.

My therapist predicted I'd engage in self-destructive behavior because I blamed myself for Kristina's death. I'd told her I hated her, so yeah, that's gonna cause some guilt. I was the last person to see her alive before she cranked up the music in her room and slammed her door.

And my therapist was right—I began to binge on drugs and alcohol and I made toxic choices in friendships and relationships. I looked forward to going to sleep each night because it was my only escape from the reality of Kristina's death.

But, somehow, I made it through those awful years. And then something amazing happened: I found comedy.

I found a new outlet for my grief.

I started to talk about Kristina.

And I *kept talking* about her.

God, now I talk about her in *everything* I do. I wrote this series called *Riley Rewind* years ago about a girl who could rewind time to try to save a classmate from committing suicide. I DIDN'T EVEN REALIZE I WAS WRITING ABOUT HER. Seriously.

I wrote movie pitches, pilots, Web series, poems, books—and everything, absolutely everything, has been about my sister. When I have enough distance from my work, I can see her there, in the cracks of everything I write. Hell, all of my YouTube videos are meant for her. Telling her all the things I've learned that she can never use. Sharing stories with her that she will never hear.

I started to talk about her suicide in videos, in podcasts, on panels, and in conversations with friends, family, even strangers. I started to make jokes about it onstage. I became an advocate for suicide prevention. It felt good to talk about what happened. Each time I did so, her death held a little less power over me. I was finally starting to heal.

What once was the most painful memory of my life soon became an aspiring one. I'd brought it out and talked about it so many times there was barely a sharp edge to it anymore.

I'VE HAD YOUNG WOMEN come up to me at the DMV, or VidCon, or at the grocery store. Sometimes they cry, other times they don't, but they have to whisper to get the words out. Sometimes it's something as simple as "Thank you" and other times it's more dramatic, like "You saved my life." I see Kristina in all of these girls. When they tell me that they wanted to kill themselves, or hurt themselves, until a video of mine changed their minds, I feel . . . well, there's really no word for that feeling.

There are times I shrug off my impact on people. It feels weird to have a friend say that I'm an "influencer" or a "role model" or even that I "make a difference." I never feel like those things. I feel like me, you know? And I don't necessarily want to feel like those things, because if I do, doesn't that make me a pompous asshole? Who goes around saying "Yes! I'm an INFLUENCER. Model your- selves after me, girls! Let *me* make a difference to *you*!"

But then there are the moments when I meet someone who cries the instant they see me, who radiates love and gratefulness. Some people hug me so tightly, crying so hard their entire body shakes, and tell me that they love me, that I've saved their lives, that I've made a difference.

These moments are hard to deny. They are why I do what I do.

Talking about Kristina and making videos that help young people has helped me heal. It's almost as if everyone I help is a hole in my own little redemption punch card. Her death no longer haunts my life—it gives me purpose.

THIS BOOK HAS NOT been easy to write. It's made me real- ize that so many of my memories are ones without Kris- tina. Every memory I'll make from February 14, 2007, on is one without her. When I turned twenty-seven, I had lived more of my life without her than with her.

There's a line I once ran across that struck me the moment I read it: "One death is a tragedy. A million deaths is a statistic." I'm not ready for Kristina to be a statistic on a teen suicide site. I'm not even ready to let her be a memory. I want people to know her, to know the brave, beautiful person she was and would have been. I want to shove her in people's faces, even if they don't get it. I'm beaming her face onto every lens and writing "Dear Kristina" at the beginning of every script.

Because Kristina is the driving force behind everything I do. This book isn't just inspired by her, it's *for* her. I want to tell her what I've learned these past ten years. I want to tell her about all the mistakes I've made—and the hard-won lessons that came out of them. Lessons about creativity, love, ambition, money, work, and everything else that felt so out of my grasp growing up. This book is filled with the advice that I would give her if she were still here, the advice I want to reach out and give to young, lost, teen girls who need it.

Most of all, I hope that Kristina, wherever she is, knows she's a part of everything I've done—and everything I will do. This book is for her.

So Much I Want to Tell You

CREATIVITY

I've spent a lot of time reading about the creative process and the different ways people work. It's a way of procrastinating that I can rationalize as "research." Once I knew I'd be writing my own book, I immediately bought every other digital influencer memoir I could get my hands on. I spent my first months of "writing time" reading, hoping that I could learn what worked and what didn't from those who set out to do this before me.

As much of a distraction as my "research" phases are, it has been useful to hear about other people's routines, rituals, and processes—and how *different* they are. I can't teach anyone how to do what they want to do, but I can tell you what works for me. In these chapters, you'll find my advice on the creative process. Take what resonates, leave what doesn't, and feel free to loosely interpret whatever you want to get what you need.

Find Your Voice

——

Most successful people will tell you to follow your dreams. I'd say *fall* into them, because I fell into mine.

After my sister died, I spent two years abusing drugs and alcohol and engaging in all that escapist won't-deal-with-my-feelings harmful stuff. LSD, MDMA, all the acronyms. But one day as I sat stoned in my room watching TV, a Comedy Central special came on. Margaret Cho was doing a routine I'd never seen before. And for the first time in a very long time, I laughed. But even better, I forgot. I forgot myself. I forgot my pain. I forgot that Kris was dead.

Seeing that show sparked something inside of me. After a couple years of feeling dead inside, I experienced joy, hope, excitement. I became obsessed with the idea of standing on a stage and making people laugh. Seeing Margaret, an Asian woman, perform stand-up gave me the confidence that I could do it too. So I took out a notebook and began to write. I wrote down every funny thing that'd ever happened to me, every funny thing I could remember saying, stories from my childhood and teenage years, thoughts and musings and random observations. I compiled a set list and performed it in front of my old DSLR camera over and over and over and over again. When I told a co-worker what I'd been doing, he said he knew a bar owner who ran a stand-up show. He asked if I wanted to get up onstage.

Uh, hell yes.

My first stand-up set was eight minutes long. Looking back, I'm always amazed. Who the hell decides to give a first-timer an eight-minute set? That's insane. Maybe if I'd realized then, I would have been more nervous. But I wasn't nervous; I was *excited*. All my friends came. My mom and dad and brother, Will, came too. Make no mistake: my jokes were terrible. They were stereotypical and cheap. I compared my first time seeing an erection to a human witnessing Godzilla. I fully acted this out with no shame or self-consciousness. But, hey, that's to be expected when you are first starting out. All that mattered was how I *felt* telling those terrible jokes. I liked being up onstage, and I wanted my writing to get better. And I loved loved *loved* the adrenaline rush that surged through me when I got a laugh.

After that night, I was hooked. I started commuting to Los Angeles from Temecula at night to do shows. It was a three-hundred-mile round-trip, but I'd practice my set in the car, sign up for the open-mic lottery at venues like the Comedy Store or the Improv, and wait to see if I got picked to go up. I did a lot of weird shows back then: shows in front of troops in their rec rooms on base, shows in coffee shops, shows in loud bars, even burlesque shows. I performed wherever I could, whether it was at an open mic, a bringer show (where you're required to bring your own paying audience in order to get onstage), or a show that someone had scraped together in the corner of a restaurant. If the show was at a bar or a club, I'd have to wait outside until it was time for my set because I was only nineteen. I'd wait until it was my turn to perform, and then a waitress or a busser or whoever would come out and escort me to the stage, let me do my set, and then kick me out.

My father and I even camped out on the sidewalk in front of the Hollywood Improv so I could audition for *Last Comic Standing*. We brought a giant pink princess tent because we thought it was hilarious. We stayed overnight, talking to the other comedians in line as I tried to choose which jokes I should tell. I didn't make it, of course. I was still so green. I remember the look of disdain on Natasha Leggero's face when she told me that I should keep working on it. I'm sure I gave her a completely oblivious look of hope and eagerness and *Yasss, Queen, I will*.

But just as I started to really find my footing, just as my jokes began to take shape, just when the lights became easier to look beyond . . . I started to *hate* doing stand-up.

I honestly didn't get it. I had loved stand-up when I

started. But then that feeling began to wane, and soon anxiety crept in. I became irrationally afraid of the stage and the audience, despite the fact that I was no longer bombing the way I had when I first started out. I wasn't necessarily great, but I definitely wasn't terrible. I was fine. Forgettable, maybe, but cute and weird. I always got at least a few laughs. So why all the crazy anxiety and dread? Why now?

If I had a show, I would *obsess* over how terrible it would go, and more often than not, I would cancel it altogether so that I could finally eat and sleep and *breathe*. I had only been doing stand-up for a year or so at this point, and I had no idea whether what I was experiencing was normal or not.

Now, thankfully, I know that it is. Some comedians will give it up, come back, give it up, come back. It's a hard craft. Even now, though I *do* stand-up, I don't feel like I *am* a stand-up comic. Stand-up is a lifestyle. The greats are, I believe, *born* to do it. I don't feel like I could ever claim that. That's something else.

My anxiety got so bad that I stopped working on my stand-up altogether. I thought about it nonstop, but I refused to get up onstage. I'd go to open-mic shows, write my name down, then quickly cross it off the list and watch the show instead. Sometimes I'd write my name down, then halfway through the open mic I would leave and drive the 150 miles back home.

I tried telling myself that it would take time. I just

needed more practice. But I couldn't do it. I couldn't eat, I couldn't sleep, I was having stomach problems, and my hair was coming out in chunks. Not even my hypnotherapist's positive affirmations could get me back onstage. (Yes, I had a hypnotherapist. It's so weird to actually write that sentence. He gave me free sessions because he dealt specifically with survivors of suicide.)

Looking back now, I can see that my anxiety stemmed from my desire to sabotage myself, to punish myself. My stage presence was getting better, my jokes were becoming more polished, and I was building a community of people who soon became friends. But I couldn't help but find a way to undermine myself. A part of my brain would whisper to me: "You don't deserve this. It's not fair that you're happy while Kristina's ashes sit in your parents' living room." I wasn't yet able to talk about Kristina's death or my pain. I wasn't able to find any light in all that darkness and it paralyzed me completely.

But that's when I found a wonderful savior, a solution for my stage fright: the Internet. Specifically, YouTube.

My brother, Will, had introduced me to YouTube years ago. He'd make these weird videos, or he and Kristina would prank me with hidden cameras and he'd upload it to his Willzorh channel. He'd shown me Ryan Higa and cat fail videos and lonelygirl15. I never really thought much about it. YouTube just seemed like a random place where you could find random stuff. I'd never thought of it as a place where you could *put* random stuff.

But in 2011, by the time I was ready to run away from the happiness that stand-up had brought me, YouTube had become *way* more of a thing. Ryan Higa now had millions of viewers. In fact, there were plenty of people with millions of views and subscribers. There were people who were making *money* from their views and subscribers. There were Web series like *The Guild,* which made Felicia Day the queen long before being geeky was cool. There were people who'd been discovered on YouTube, like Justin Bieber, people who were now famous.

Yes, I thought. Yes, this is for me! Stand-up is all about lights, people, a microphone. Nightclubs and bars and drinks after the midnight show. But YouTube? YouTube's got *homebody* written all over it: staying inside by yourself, not having to deal with anyone, editing and cringing at your face onscreen until you're somewhat happy with the result. Never having to leave your house. Using your cat as a background element. Uploading your finished product to the Internet and never dealing with the reality of a live audience.

The fact that I could now perform without a live audience set me on *fire*. I had so many ideas! I decided to hold myself to a schedule: no matter what, I would make at least one video every week.

When I first started, videos came easily. There were so many things I wanted to talk about: How I'd always believed that when I turned sixteen I'd have a superpower, and how adulthood felt like a sham. How I wanted to kill the inner Internet troll inside of my head that was my worst enemy. My conflicted feelings about being a home-body. I reenacted fantasies I had when I was younger, like wanting to be a spy and practicing witchcraft in middle school.

Making these videos was fun. I loved playing around with the most basic visual effects, buying props and doing set design, creating makeshift costumes out of what I had lying around the house. I'd spend a day writing a bunch of scripts, then film for the next day or two, and conclude the week with editing and any visual effect work. I was a one-woman show. I came to love the seemingly endless freedom that YouTube provided.

Once I blew through the more superficial topics, though, I was forced to write more personal, deeper stories. I started talking about my social anxiety, my struggle with organized religion, and stories about random encounters in my life. That run-in with the guy on the elevator who wouldn't move, the awkward confrontation with someone who hit my parked car and walked away. Anytime I experienced something relatively interesting or morally conflicting, I made a video about it. YouTube became my diary, and making videos became a form of catharsis. I would go to therapy to discuss my latest struggle, and then I'd go home and make a video to reinforce whatever advice my therapist offered that resonated with me. It became a way for me to document various chapters in my life, get closure on certain issues, and hold myself accountable.

The first time I ever talked about Kristina on camera

was hard. Editing the video was harder. Uploading it was the worst. I wasn't sure what people were going to say. I worried about being judged for talking about something so private in public. But I'd gotten to a point where it was something I *wanted* to talk about. YouTube videos had become such a natural way of expressing myself that I wanted to dive deeper and talk about something that really mattered. *Please Don't Kill Yourself* was a video that I made for those who are suicidal. If there's anything that I knew, it was how broken suicide left the people who remained. And I wanted to make something that maybe if my sister had seen it, it would've changed her mind. The reception was mixed: some people thanked me for it, but others insisted that suicide is a personal choice. Either way, I felt a huge sense of relief over finally putting it out there. It was a relief to not just mention her suicide in passing but to really express how much her death had fucked up my family.

MY VIDEO-MAKING PROCESS HAS evolved a lot over the years, but by now I've landed on what really works for me. I always start with a topic: something I'm passionate about, or interested in exploring, or something that makes me angry or sad.

Then I find a title. The perfect title is one that encapsulates what the video is about. There's nothing worse than a clickbait title that has nothing to do with the content you're watching. A title sets up your audience's expectations. It's your thesis statement, your logline, your promise about what you're going to deliver. The best titles also imply that the audience is going to learn something, whether it's a video like *Who Is a Slut?*, in which I conclude that the only person who can label someone as a slut is themselves (after analyzing their own sexual motivations), or a satirical comedy like *How to Not Get Raped,* where I explore the vast amount of information given to women about avoiding physical violence in comparison to the little time spent teaching men about consent.

Next, I write a script. My videos are always structured as long monologues with cutaways to either (a) demonstrate or emphasize a point, (b) directly oppose it for the sake of a joke, or (c) answer a posed question.

Two and a half years into making Internet videos, I had hundreds of thousands of subscribers. I would write furiously in my journal each day, eager to remember whatever emotional upset I was going through so I could turn it into my weekly video. I spent a lot of time self-reflecting, trying to psychoanalyze my own behavior. I mined my past experiences for ideas: the middle school mistake of cutting my own bangs, dealing with beauty image issues, how often I did the wrong thing in a relationship and tended to overreact to the smallest things.

The more videos I made, the stronger my creative voice became. And as my self-knowledge grew, so did my confidence. I had a point of view. I had specific opinions on so many topics. I was a girl who loved cats and prop guns and who would offer advice on the Internet about love and friendship and self-discipline. That was me. After wandering around aimlessly for so many years, I'd felt like I'd found my voice—and myself.

Once You've Found Your Voice, Let It Evolve

—

I have a lot of respect for anyone who creates content on the regular. Even daily vloggers. *Especially* daily vloggers. If it were easy, everyone would do it. But it's not. You get tired. You get burnt out. You realize it's all way more work than you thought it would be—making sure you are always doing something new and interesting, sifting through footage, spending hours editing and animating text or visual effects. It's *hard*. It starts to feel like you're on a hamster wheel, that you must constantly produce new content or die of irrelevancy.

By 2014, I'd made over 150 YouTube videos. I loved making them, but I was beginning to wonder if I had made my video topics too broad. I'd spend two and a half minutes distilling a complex topic down to something digestible and comedic, but that meant I'd blown through material. Entire topics of depression and anxiety had a single two-minute video devoted to them already. Making another felt like I was doubling back or duplicating material. I'd gone through topic after topic, and I found myself feeling empty, like I'd run out of things to say.

Somewhere along the way, I decided to try my hand at creating short films and more sketch-based comedy. As much as I loved making my weekly comedic videos, my heart was always with narrative content. I was an actor first, but the world knew me only as the girl on YouTube. I realized I wanted to change that.

By this time I had built my subscriber base to over a million. But when I started to explore new formats, my viewership began to decrease, and I frantically scrambled to produce more videos in the style I was best known for: videos in which I offered personal advice and acted out all the parts. I went back and forth like this for a year—wanting to please my audience, but also wanting to fulfill myself creatively. In the end, my creative needs won out.

Sometimes I wonder if I've made a mistake. I've seen other YouTubers skyrocket past me, boasting seven million subscribers, with each of their videos raking in millions of views. I worry that my decision to move toward sketch comedy and short films rather than stick to vlogging cost me a lot of my viewers. I worry that taking on brand deals to pay for the six short films I did in 2014 took a bigger toll on my audience retention than I'd anticipated. People got bored; they left. This wasn't what they signed up for. They wanted the girl with the cats and the clones and the guns, the girl who told stories and gave advice.

That's what I hear from a lot of young girls who come up to me: "I miss your old videos, where you gave advice." Then, when they see the look of horror on my face, they quickly add, "The sketch stuff and short films are cool too."

But then I realize I didn't make a mistake. Trying new things is the best thing I can do for myself as an artist. In fact, it's the best thing any artist can do. It's always hard. And you fail hard a lot of the time. But if you're not failing, you're not learning. Yes, perhaps changing things up meant losing some of my subscribers. But the lessons I learned about myself and my craft were invaluable. Ultimately, I did exactly what I had set out to do: I proved that I could do more than just make short videos about my own life. I had put myself through my own film school, and now I had a portfolio of directing and acting work that I could showcase.

One of the hardest things about being an artist is finding the balance between staying true to your voice and allowing yourself room to evolve. How do you push yourself out of your comfort zone while still trying to create art that feels commercially relevant? How do you balance learning new skills and trying new things with still keeping your core fan base happy?

It's a tricky balancing act, and I'm not sure if I've mastered it quite yet. I have a tendency to want to do *too* many things, often spreading my focus—and myself—too thin. I wonder where I'd be now if I'd stuck to doing just one thing. I'm such a multi-hyphenate that meetings can get confusing. People are always trying to figure me out: So you do stand-up? And you act? And you have a clothing line? And you do YouTube?

These days, I don't obsess over subscriber numbers like I used to. I'll skim through the comments on the days I post videos, but I don't try to read each one. Now I just try to make stuff that's truthful. Stuff that I care about. And stuff that's funny. I want to say something while making people laugh or think. That's my voice. That's my "brand."

The creative process is exactly that: a process. Every time you make something, you learn something. Most of what I've learned has come from the mistakes I've made— like when I've had to reshoot an entire clone scene or completely rewrite my monologue because the improvisation I did in the cutaways renders the whole thing nonsensical.

Sometimes people ask me: "Are you ever worried you'll run out of ideas?" *Yes.* The answer is always yes. I've made nearly three hundred monologue videos and I feel like I've articulated every opinion I have. Some weeks it's a struggle to think of what else I possibly have to say. And then there are topics I desperately want to talk about but don't necessarily feel qualified to. LGBTQ+, for example. Or Black Lives Matter. Or how hard it must be for Muslim Americans in this political climate. These are messages and causes I am passionate about but have no substantial life experience to speak from.

Yes, I worry that I will run out of ideas every time I sit down to think of a new video. Every time I upload a new video, I worry it will be my last. But here's the thing: you'll only run out of ideas if you close yourself off to things—to new ideas, new experiences, new people. Don't be afraid to change, to grow, and to learn—that's the only way to keep yourself creatively vital.

If You Want to Be the Star, Create the Show

—

When I was twenty-one, I moved to Los Angeles to start my acting career.

On my first night in LA, I bought a bottle of wine at the liquor store down the street from my new apartment and drank it alone in celebration. I had no idea what I was doing, but I still felt like I was living the dream.

To be honest, I was a terrible actor when I first started. I'd done a few high school plays, but I had no formal training. Like many aspiring actors, I assumed I had a natural talent that would kick in once I got in front of a casting director. During my first audition for a play I quickly realized I was mistaken. I was shaking so hard that the paper rattling in my hands was making more noise than the lines coming out of my mouth.

But my lack of talent didn't deter me. After all, my father had always taught me that if you worked hard enough, it would pay off. I figured I needed to take every opportunity to act that I could. That was the only way I was going to get better.

I took an acting class, which was a great starting place, but the workshop format meant only acting for about ten to twenty minutes and sitting in a chair for the next three and a half hours. I couldn't afford to be in more than one acting class. I couldn't control how many auditions I got. I grew frustrated with the countless self-submissions I did on online casting sites that led nowhere. How was I going to get better at acting if there were no opportunities to actually act? When the majority of your career is auditioning more than actually working, honing your craft feels impossible.

At the time I was working several jobs just to make ends meet. In the mornings I worked in a chiropractor's office scheduling appointments and doing administrative work. After that I would head to a sushi restaurant, where I had a five-hour lunch shift. In the evenings I worked odd Craigslist jobs that never lasted long: a gig as a host in a Koreatown cocktail bar where married men came for company, a cocktail waitress in an underground poker club, a dog walker for a retired police officer who constantly asked me to stay for dinner. Then I'd go home to my three cats and three gay roommates. Ah, what a time.

In 2012, a manager who had encouraged me early on to take acting classes left to become an agent and agreed to sign me. Soon I was auditioning for TV shows. I was twenty-two, but I looked like I was fourteen, so I mostly went in for roles on the Disney Channel and for high school shows on MTV. I booked my first gig on the show *Awkward,* a one-line part in which I yelled in Japanese about how big Ashley Rickards's boobs were.

Over the next two years I booked roles here and there. But the only parts I ever landed involved quick one-liners—and I usually booked these parts only because I misinterpreted the material, providing the casting directors with a refreshing take on something they'd heard a million times before. I was discouraged: I wanted bigger parts. I wanted to have an arc on something.

While I was auditioning for roles and working my various odd jobs, I had also started my YouTube channel and my audience had grown significantly. In 2012, I was at half a million subscribers and counting. But back then the traditional entertainment industry looked down on digital influencers. They hadn't yet recognized our built-in audiences as powerful marketing tools. Even after I reached a million subscribers and YouTubers began to get cast in digital company movies left and right, I still felt like I had little control over the parts I wanted to play. I was auditioning for the nerdy best friend who would be upset over a B-minus, the hacker or technologically savvy team player, or a hypersexualized accented foreigner.

I wanted to be the lead. I was tired of feeling powerless in my career.

That's when I decided to start making my own stuff.

The first series I wrote was called *Riley Rewind,* which

focused on a time-traveling teen trying to save a classmate from suicide. My partner at the time loved the idea, and we decided to produce it together—he would direct, I would act—and we released it on his channel. The reaction to the series was amazing. *Variety* named us one of the top Web series of the year. We had over twenty million cumulative views. The fans connected with the concept and really liked the animated elements.

But *Riley* was expensive to make, and while we sold it to Netflix and other various video-on-demand services, it still lost money. My partner had paid for it out of his own pocket, and we soon realized that this wasn't a sustainable business model.

A few years went by. Auditions came and went. I still did my regular YouTube videos, but nothing as substantial as *Riley.* It was still the work I was most proud of. I wanted to do more like it. So two years later, in 2014, I decided to take on brand deals in order to raise the money to create more content.

I was transparent with my audience: I told them I wanted to try something new and I needed money to do it. I put sponsored messaging at the end of my regular comedy videos, and once the paycheck came in, I had a budget.

The first short I made was *Hallucination,* a psychological thriller about a girl with schizophrenia who confronts her hallucinations. I debated whether or not to play the lead part. This would be my first time directing a crew, and I wasn't quite sure how it was going to play out. In the end, I decided to cast an actor—a good friend of mine, Alexis—as the lead.

My team was skeletal, to put it generously: a producer, a director of photography, a few grips/gaffers, sound. The shoot took a mere day, and it was my first time directing a crew. I was addicted. I loved the energy of being on a set, of framing a shot and talking to actors. My decision to cast Alexis paid off. I had been so busy with directing that acting simultaneously would've been impossible. She brought my writing to life beautifully.

Though I told my audience I was aiming to make one short film a month, once I started I realized how impossible that was. I made six short films total that year—*Hallucination, Emergency Call, Afflicted Inc., PREG-NAPOCALYPSE, Here She Is,* and *Miss Earth.* Making these was one of the most difficult yet rewarding things I'd ever done. I'd be writing one, in pre-production for another, and editing a third all at the same time. I was constantly in all four stages of production, all the while also maintaining my weekly video deadline.

At the end of 2014, I got word that *Miss Earth* was being picked up to series by go90. We'd have a *big* budget. Bigger than anything I'd ever worked with. I'd be sur-rounded by a team of traditional writers and directors and crew. And I'd get to be the lead. *Miss Earth* became *Miss 2059.* I was the star of a series and an executive producer for the show. We shot for twenty consecutive days, and I got a real look at what it takes to lead a show.

Making my own stuff was the best thing I ever did for my career. It gave me a sense of control, allowed me the opportunity to get better at my craft, and offered me creative freedom to try new things. If I want to make a short film about every woman in the world getting pregnant by alien invasion, who's going to stop me? I can walk into audition rooms without feeling like I desperately need to book a part that I don't actually want. Why should I? I'm making my own stuff. I'm busy as shit giving myself roles I like. I don't have to take every opportunity thrown my way. I can pick and choose. It's a beautiful and fortunate place to be, and I am grateful for it.

More important, making my own films means I don't have to be trapped by typecasting. I don't have to play the best friend, the hacker, the overly studious girl terrified of getting a B on a final. If I'm writing and directing and producing and acting and editing and funding and *creating* the damn thing, no one can tell me where I fit into the narrative. I am the motherfucking narrative.

That's why I tell anyone who will listen—especially girls—to make your own stuff. God, please make your own stuff. You don't need a million subscribers or billions of views. Look at the success of *Broad City*—those girls started out with a small, low-budget Web series with barely any views. But Amy Poehler saw it, and now it's one of the best comedies on TV.

You just need the right person to see your work. And even if that doesn't happen for a long, long time, you'll be a better creator for it. You'll have found and developed your voice, gained knowledge of the technical and creative side of filmmaking, and kept yourself busy doing something you love. It will be hard. It will be frustrating. It will feel like you're throwing something into a black hole. But will it hurt? No. You have so much to gain and nothing to lose.

If you want to be the star, create the show. Don't wait. Make your own opportunities. There's no better time to start than today.

The Only Way to Start Is to Start

———

'm constantly asked: "What advice do you have for people who want to do what you do?" and "How do I get
started?" I wish I had a great answer to these questions.

There must be some secret, I think. There must be
some life hack or magic word that other artists have stum-
bled upon. But the truth is, I know that that's not the case.
I know the answer is much simpler than that.

The answer is the action. If you want to do stand-up,
you have to write jokes and get on a stage. If you want to
make YouTube videos, you buy a camera and press record.
If you want to be an actor, you take acting classes and try
to audition for anything you can.

It's so simple, but the majority of us overthink it. We
waste time researching the thing we want to do, instead of
actually doing it.

I've been doing comedy for seven years: stand-up,

sketch, improv, videos. I am lucky enough to have had a military father who instilled self-discipline and a solid work ethic in me. My ingrained love for scheduling and organization has also been a godsend. Deciding to do something is the easy part. The hard part is finding the time to do it, and then to keep doing it.

The best way to combat laziness or discouragement is to create a routine. Your body will soon begin to follow the routine naturally, as will your mind. Most successful people I know have been setting aside time for their work since they were young. The beautiful thing is that it's never too late to start!

Don't underestimate the power of decision. Once you decide to do something, that it's something you *must* do, you'll make time for it. You'll find a way to start, even if you don't have professional filming equipment or screen-writing software. All the time you spend wondering how to do something could be spent actually doing it—and getting better at it.

So the next time you ask yourself "How do I start?" maybe rephrase the question to *"When* am I going to start?"

The answer is now.

It's Called Work
for a Reason

—

So let's say you've set aside one hour every day to write. Great! You've started. Congratulations.

Now you sit in front of your computer, staring at a blank page. The entire hour goes by and you've written nothing. So you try again, and again, but every time you write something, the words are clunky, awkward, and you can't figure out what you want to write about.

You're doing great.

I used to believe that creation came easily to artistic geniuses. That everything they made was a masterpiece. Now I know that's not true.

No one creates something worthwhile without putting in the work and the time. We can't passively wait around for inspiration to hit or for the muse to show up. So even if you sit in front of the computer for hours, with nothing to show for it, don't get discouraged. Keep up the habit.

Making time for creativity in your day will also make space for it in your mind. It'll keep it at the top of your subconscious to-do list while you're going about the rest of your day. Eventually your muse will appear.

If you're feeling extra motivated, making *results* a part of your to-do list instead of a *time commitment* also helps. So instead of saying that you'll write for an hour, you can always say you'll write a minimum of five hundred words. They might be the shittiest five hundred words you've ever written, but you'll be five hundred closer to some you like.

Ideas Are a
Dime a Dozen

I find it strange when people ask where ideas come from. As if Stephen King is going to point to a well in the ground and say, "There. All my ideas come from there."

Ideas aren't that hard to find. They mostly come from stimulation and thinking. Read books, watch TV, explore the world around you. Take walks and think about bringing two seemingly random concepts together. Be observant: pay attention to how people interact and to what's going on in the world.

Write "what if" lists. These lists are where most of my short film ideas have come from. *Hallucination:* What if a girl with schizophrenia confronted her hallucination? *Afflicted, Inc.:* What if personal afflictions like anorexia or bipolar disorder were actually saleswomen from an alternate universe? Playing "what if" can generate thousands of ideas, and eventually you'll stumble onto one that will resonate.

What's more important than knowing where ideas come from is knowing when an idea is bad. I've wasted months of my life writing novels that have terrible premises. *Schizophrenic Lesbian in Space* was a 400,000-word odyssey that I worked on every day for National Novel Writing Month.

But even though an initial idea might be bad, that doesn't mean that it can't become something good. *Schizophrenic Lesbian in Space* eventually transformed into the pilot for *Miss Earth,* a tale of twins who are swapped in an intergalactic competition. It's *Miss Congeniality* meets *The Hunger Games,* set in space. It's by far one of my best projects to date.

Keep track of your ideas—the good ones, the bad ones, the ones that make no sense. You can always change them to suit your needs. Yesterday's cringeworthy idea may become the premise for a fantastic series tomorrow.

It's Okay if
It Sucks

—

First drafts. Early videos. There will come a day when you throw up your hands and wonder if anything you make is ever going to *not* suck. Will anything be any good?

I still feel like most of what I put out could be better. Occasionally I make a video and contemplate whether or not to upload it because I hate it so much. But I've learned that it's all a part of the process. Not everything you make can be gold. But every terrible thing you make will get you one step closer to making something better.

Whenever I make something, I try to learn at least one thing from the process. Just one thing that will make the next thing better. There is always room for improvement. It's easy to obsess over the fact that what you've made is not good, but you'll be better off if you try to learn from the experience. Analyze *why* something sucks and *how* you can do better, rather than focusing on the negative.

I knew I wasn't the strongest writer when I began creating short films. I knew I needed to put a lot of work in if I was going to get any better. I also began to notice that whenever I directed *and* acted in something, my acting suffered. I was too focused on directing to fully commit to the character.

I've found that sometimes it's helpful to give yourself permission to suck. It just takes the pressure off. For example, when I was doing improvisation, we used to play a game called Bad Improv. It's a warm-up exercise where everyone is allowed to break all the rules and be terrible improvisers. You can run into another person's scene screaming "I'm a fucking ghost!" and you'll be winning at Bad Improv. The thing is, Bad Improv can be pretty funny. It's a good reminder that sometimes you can get distracted by the "right" way to do something.

So the next time you cringe at something you've created, don't shut down. First, take a breath. Try to detach yourself from it emotionally. Assess your work analytically. Become aware of your weaknesses and focus on improving them—that's the only way you'll get stronger. And the stronger you get, the more resilient you'll become.

Fail More

—

All successful people have a trail of failures behind them. We're a culture that shames failing, but trial and error is an essential part of any process (and life in general). We learn from our mistakes: from experimenting and attempting and trying. There's nothing wrong with failing—in fact, it's a good sign. You're one step closer to succeeding.

I had a callback to a Melissa McCarthy movie. I was sitting in the waiting room with the other girls, listening to the explosion of laughter that would come from the audition room. I was nervous. Melissa McCarthy was in there! And she was going to read her character's lines with me! I was also nervous because a notable comedy casting director, Allison Jones, had brought me straight into a producer session for this role (meaning it was the first time I was reading the material out loud for the producers; normally you have an initial audition before a callback with them). I always get nervous when I'm brought straight into a callback. I like the initial audition process. You get a chance to read the character with the casting director and be guided by them. By the time you get to the callback, you have a better hold on your performance.

But this was a role I hadn't read for. I had no idea who this character was, and I was a little confused about what made her funny. When it was my turn, I went in the room and did my best.

And I failed so fucking hard.

I wasn't funny. There were no laughs. I could feel myself slowly crashing and burning in front of everyone's eyes. I wanted to melt into the floor and disappear. Here I was, in front of comedy legend Melissa McCarthy, and I wasn't even remotely funny. I left the audition and banged my head against the wheel of my car. I beat myself up the whole way home.

Then there was the time I had to pitch a comic book to a studio in hopes of getting a graphic novel under my belt. I hate pitching. For those of you who don't know, pitching is basically telling a story, conversationally, to an executive. You describe the movie or TV show or comic book and its characters and what the story looks like from beginning to end. I hate it. I'm terrible at communicating stories in person. I skip ahead and explain things badly. I'm always tempted to just read my notes, but people want you to pitch with your voice and charisma, and to lead them with your energy. Unfortunately, it's not my strong suit. I'm bad at talking to people I like at parties. It's going to take me a long time to get good at talking to executives who can fund my projects.

So there I was, in front of the executives, rambling on about the world and the story and the characters. Finally I got to the end. I felt good about it. I'd practiced this pitch out loud at home for an hour. I'd even recorded myself on my phone and listened to it, noting where I'd improvised nicely and where I was stale.

Finally the executive said, "I'm so confused."

Confusion is worse than someone not liking your story. Because they don't even understand what the hell your story is about.

While neither of these experiences was fun, they are ones that I'll live with and learn from. I know what I did wrong, so hopefully next time I can do it right. Failure is so many wonderful things; it's motivation to do better next time, a learning opportunity to see what you did wrong, and ultimately the proof that you at least *tried*. So many people are afraid of failure that it stops them from ever trying. Instead of feeling ashamed over failures, we should embrace them. They're a necessary evil. And though I will still cringe in embarrassment each time one of these memories is brought to the surface, I still give my-self a little pat on the back for the attempt, and I silently vow to do better next time.

You Are Not
Your Art

—

Artists have a tendency to value themselves in relation to their work. If I'm creating content that people love, I'm happy. If I have a video that isn't well received, I'm destroyed. This is a very unproductive and distracting way to work. Though I haven't fully mastered it yet, I'm becoming better at detaching my self-worth from what I create.

I am not my art, I tell myself.

I am not this two-minute video about how much I hate the phrase "over my dead body." I am not this rap song about how I treat my boyfriend when I'm hungry. I am not this book.

Instead, I try to find my value in what I'm doing for people and the world. In who I am in my everyday life. In what my actions say about the kind of person I am. My life is defined by what I do in the here and now—not by what I create.

Develop a
Thick Skin

—

I've had a complicated relationship with trolls. I used to read each and every single comment on my videos, looking for advice that might help me with my next video. But the majority of comments on YouTube are extreme. Some people unconditionally love what you do or who you are and will support you no matter what. Though it's a fantastic feeling, it doesn't necessarily help you improve your work. Then there are the "haters," as they're called. These people insult your appearance, work, family, and self-worth.

These hateful comments used to get to me. I've cried. I've responded. I've fought with some and ignored others. I've tried engaging in meaningful and constructive conversations. I've tried one-upping their insults. I've tried not looking at the comments until a video is days old, when the urge to respond to comments has lost most of its power.

Every artist has to decide how to deal with the criticism. I used to indulge my self-pity and self-hatred by looking myself up on Reddit and crying when I found what was waiting for me there. But now I've learned not to read comments if I'm having a bad day.

I've also come to appreciate the fact that the Internet's vitriol has forced me to develop a thick skin. People are a thousand times crueler when they are hiding behind the anonymity of a screen and a keyboard. I've read the words "you're a talentless cunt" more times than I can count. The comments online are so bad that I'm now able to shrug off anything mildly rude in real life. I've heard worse.

Don't misunderstand me. I don't think that cruel comments are a good thing. But I've taken to imagining who is on the other end of the keyboard, and that helps me deal with all the negative aspects of being a female online. The person making nasty comments is probably a teenager, I tell myself. A teenager who just learned how to use cusswords. Or some sad, lonely person who wants to take out their anger on someone they don't know from the safety of their home. Thinking about who these trolls actually are puts the objectification, the degradation, and the endless cruelty into perspective. And I've become a stronger person as a result.

———

There you have it. These are some of the things I've learned as a creative person over the last seven years. Though it's not always easy to implement them, they're a gentle reminder that you're doing just fine. It's all part of the process. Enjoy the journey. I am.

2

IDENTITY

It's never easy to feel comfortable in your own skin, or happy all the time, but knowing who you are and what you believe in is the first step toward taking control of your life.

When It Comes to Self-Care, Find What Works for You

––––

was very depressed after my sister died. And I had good reason to be. But mental health was a topic rarely discussed (or even acknowledged) in my family. So instead of talking about my feelings with a therapist or going to see a doctor, I self-medicated. I drank lots of alcohol, smoked weed, and took mushrooms, LSD, MDMA. I consumed whatever I could to forget the questions constantly circling around in my head: Would I ever see her again? Was she out there somewhere? Or was she just gone?

These questions tormented me when I was sober. So I refused to be sober.

Being in mourning means crying until you've got nothing left. It means sitting with sadness until you're so sick of it you can't feel sad anymore. I didn't want to do that. I wanted to alter my mind and think of other things and forget Kristina Marie Akana ever existed.

My depression became so bad that I started taking drugs by myself. I didn't go anywhere; I was always home. I have no idea if my parents knew what I was doing. I thought my mom must have known, because I once crawled down the stairs and flopped onto her while she watched TV, but maybe she just assumed I was being cuddly. After all, my parents have never done drugs. How would they know that this burst of affection and love was the result of a pill?

I enrolled in community college, but I often skipped class to get high. I became horribly shy to the point where I couldn't talk to strangers. In an attempt to get my life back on track, I interned at a veterinary practice to see if I wanted to go into animal science. But I spent most of the days in the corner, refusing to speak unless someone spoke directly to me. It was impossible to make new friends.

Before Kristina died I'd had a job at GameStop, but I took time off after her death. When I eventually returned to work, it was a disaster. I'd often break down and cry in the backroom. Working a dead-end job, going through the motions at community college, and drinking/smoking myself into oblivion made up the entirety of my life. Gone was the ambition to be a military officer, a veterinarian, anything at all. Though I'd always secretly dreamed of a career in acting and writing, these dreams felt as dead and unattainable to me as my sister did.

In those years, I smoked weed five times a day. I eventually quit my job at GameStop and started working at a pizza place. I'd smoke before work, clean the place like crazy until my high wore off, then get high during my lunch break and continue scrubbing the ovens. I'd get high when I got home and play videogames. Then I'd get high and go to bed. On some nights I'd take harder drugs by myself and cry. Other nights I'd take drugs with friends, but I might as well have been alone.

I also got addicted to eBay and buried myself in $10,000 worth of debt. Buying things made me feel good. It made me feel alive, at least temporarily. I would shoplift random things here and there just for the thrill of it. My heart would race as I snuck a pair of clip-on earrings I'd never wear into my bag—it felt *so good*.

I have no idea what the rest of my family was doing during this period of my life. Once in a while I'd hear Mom crying in her room at night. I'd turn up my music, not wanting to join her in the endless crying that seemed to dominate our life. I'd see my brother, Will, around the house, but we didn't talk much. He seemed just as numb as me, but without the reliance on substances. My father was lost in World of Warcraft, gaming away his pain in fantasyland.

When I found comedy and stand-up, I found my motivation. I finally realized that my purposelessness was only fueling my depression and drug use. So I dove into performing and acting and never looked back. I replaced MDMA with the high of walking onstage. I didn't need acid; Hollywood was enough of a trip.

Although I finally stopped taking drugs and abusing alcohol, my depression never went away completely. It was different from what I'd suffered when my sister died, though. It wasn't as sharp or raw. It was dull. A sort of bland blanket of pain that covered everything. I'd think, *Even if my career is everything I want it to be, does it matter? We all die. Nothing matters.* I isolated myself in my office and at home with my cats. I became a work-aholic, rarely engaging with anything I didn't deem pro-ductive or professionally beneficial.

I'd lost the ability to connect with people. I'd sit and stare at them when there was a lull in conversation, like I'd completely forgotten how to be a human being. People would ask me, "How are you?" and I wouldn't know how to respond. At least when my sister died, I'd felt so much rage and sadness that it was impossible to ignore. Now things felt so bland. *How am I? I don't know. My career is fine. My friends are fine. My love life is fine. I feel like I'm on this hamster wheel of never-ending work, chasing this idea of "making it" that intellectually I know doesn't exist. I know that we all die, so why am I wasting so much time working? Why am I chasing a feeling that I know I'll never have?* I didn't have the answers to these questions—and I still don't.

And it makes me unhappy. It makes me sad. It makes me lie on the floor and stare at the ceiling and think of nothing.

For several years, my therapist suggested I try anti-depressants. I always politely declined, insisting that I'd rather try holistic methods like exercise, vitamins, vegan diets, etc. For a while, this seemed to work. As long as I was immersed in my work and adhering to a strict routine, I didn't notice my depression too much. It stayed in the background, muted and unimportant. As long as I ignored my anxiety or drowned it in alcohol during social events, I was fine. If I was struggling to get my work done, I'd lie down and imagine the moment of my death to try to urge myself to get back to the things I had to do.

When I finally decided to try antidepressants, I was motivated by a variety of things: my therapist's continued urging, my worsening depression and anxiety, the fact that I was becoming an impossible person to live with. But the main reason I decided to try them was because I knew I was being a hypocrite.

I'd been a fierce advocate for destigmatizing mental illness and I'd been vocal on YouTube and on social media about suicide prevention. There I was, preaching to the masses every day, but I couldn't even take my own therapist's advice.

Looking back now, I think my reluctance to take antidepressants had to do with the fact that to do so would mean I'd have to acknowledge my depression was real. And that scared me. It somehow felt like defeat. But I realized that I was perpetuating the very stereotypes I was arguing against. So I did what I always do when I'm going to make a decision and want to hold myself accountable: I made a video. That way I couldn't back down. I told my audience that I'd been a hypocrite and that I'd be starting medication.

Then I went to see my doctor.

I explained to him my reluctance to go on too high a dose and my fears of potential addiction. He nodded along, exasperated in the non-condescending but tired way that is unique to doctors. He asked about my family history. I told him about my sister's suicide and the history of addiction that ran in my family—gambling, alcohol, and online gaming.

He nodded, made a note in his folder, and asked me about my habits. Did I exercise regularly? Yes. Eat healthy? Yes. Get enough sleep? Yes. Did I handle stress well? Not really, but I was working on it.

Finally he asked about my symptoms. I told him about how often I'd lie on the floor, the feeling of hopelessness, the anxiety that kept me home, my fatigue and irritability.

My doctor decided to do blood work before prescribing any medication. He wanted to rule out any thyroid issues, potential anemia, or whatever else there might be. He drew some blood and said he would call when he got the results.

A week later he called. Everything looked fine. There was nothing wrong with me physically. So I went back in to talk about antidepressants. Again I explained to him my fears of going on medication. How I'd heard horror stories of foggy heads and weight gain. How people said their entire world turned dull and without color. I said I wanted to go on the lowest possible dose. He sighed and put my medical folder down.

"I have high blood pressure," he said. "That runs in my

family. It's genetic. If I don't take my blood pressure medication, I suffer. So I take it. Will I die without it? No. But it makes my life a lot easier. You have depression. Based on what you've told me about your family history, it most likely runs in your family."

I nodded. It made sense. It was just an illness like any other.

"Will medication cure your depression? No. But it'll make your life a little easier."

In that moment, it clicked for me. Though I'd spent years talking about the stigma against mental illness, I'd never fully internalized it on an emotional level. Intellectually, it made sense. But it was so ingrained in me that I hadn't even realized I was perpetuating it against myself.

The biggest difference between mental and physical illness is the differing attitudes people have toward them. If you have the flu, cancer, or a broken bone, family and friends are right there with you, caring for you and eager to help. But when we talk about schizophrenia, bipolar disorder, or clinical depression, it's a different story.

I went on 10 mg of Lexapro. Though the four-week transition period was rough (fatigue, sleepiness, walking through a fog), I quickly felt a change. Gone was the dull blanket covering my brain. My step felt lighter. My mind felt lighter. I didn't react to life's events with such intense anger or sadness.

Oh, I thought. This is what mental and emotional clarity feels like.

It was as if my whole life up until this moment had

been lived on a roller coaster—consisting of extreme ups and downs, loops at top speed, and abrupt, unforeseen stops. Going on Lexapro made me feel like I was riding first class on a luxurious train. Everything was smooth. I was able to enjoy the sights. I was able to breathe easily and think in peace and quiet.

Lexapro did not "fix" or "cure" my depression. It was just the final boost I needed. All my other lifestyle choices—exercising regularly, eating healthy, building a support system—were hugely important when it came to managing my depression. But the effects of going on medication changed my life. I became enthusiastic about bringing it up in conversation. Whenever someone asked, "How are you?" I'd immediately dive into my experience with antidepressants, hoping that someone else had experienced the same thing. I was surprised at how many of my friends and colleagues were on ADs. I had conversations with Uber drivers and waiters about their own struggles with depression. It was so much more common than I'd ever realized.

Why didn't anyone talk about this stuff?

Although I was thrilled that the medication was working, some of my friends and family were not supportive. Some warned me against the "fake happiness" that ADs gave you. I was urged to find happiness inside myself instead of over the counter. Several friends of mine told me that they'd tried antidepressants but the side effects had been too much for them. I heard stories of how some medications randomly stopped being effective. My parents gave me a giant bag of vitamins and assured me that depression would go away with old age.

I listened to everyone and registered their concerns, but in the end, I knew what was best for me and I stayed on the Lexapro. When it comes to any kind of self-care, you have to find what works for you. We all have different bodies, minds, and attitudes. What works for one person won't necessarily work for another. And the regimen you find for yourself might someday change.

It took me too long to face up to my own prejudices and fears surrounding mental health. When I was finally able to acknowledge that I was a walking contradiction and take full ownership of my depression, I found the missing piece of the puzzle I'd been searching for. I'm certainly not happy all the time, and I will always struggle with depression and anxiety, but deciding to take medication changed my life for the better—and I hope my story empowers people to take charge of their own well-being.

Succeed Because of Your Race, Not Despite It

—

I didn't realize I was Asian until I was eight.

I can't remember who pointed it out to me. But once I knew, it became hard to ignore. I started noticing just how little Asian representation there was onscreen. Who were my Asian role models growing up? Jackie Chan? Lucy Liu? That's it?

Growing up, my family spent a lot of time overseas or in small towns in the United States, mostly on military bases. My dad was a naval flight officer, my mother a homemaker with three kids. We moved every two to three years to a new state or country. By the time I was six, I'd already been to thirteen states. My parents loved sightseeing, experiencing different cultures, and trying new food. I was always surrounded by Caucasian kids and I never really considered myself any different from them. No one ever treated me differently, at least.

I didn't encounter racism until our move to Temecula, California (which, for a city in an area known for its wine and hot-air balloons, has a lot of racial tension).

My first day as a junior at Chaparral High School, I was told: "Go back to China, chink!" I stared at the weird white guy with platinum-blond buzzed hair and said, "I'm Japanese." He spit in my direction and walked away.

After that, racism continued to play a role in my life, but I didn't let it affect me. People can call you names, they can assume stereotypes are true, they can be assholes. None of that mattered. Until I started acting. What mattered then was the very real but invisible wall that came down between me and my career because of my race.

My theater program in high school was the usual group of misfits: mostly horny white kids who liked classic movies and musicals and plays. They were all pretty accepting of me, and I never really clashed with any of them.

My drama teacher, on the other hand, was a different story. He had tried to make it in Hollywood as a Latino actor. But he was only able to book stereotypical Latino roles (Gangster #3, for instance) and found it too discouraging, so he left LA and became a teacher in Temecula. Now, I have nothing against him or the path he chose. I think everyone has to do what they feel is right in their life. I don't think toughing it out in a career your heart isn't in is the right way to live. But he was clearly angry at the way the industry had treated him and he took it out on his students, telling me that I'd never make it in Hollywood because I was Asian.

I've always been kind of stupid when it comes to color. When a friend of mine and I co-directed a Christmas play for our drama class, we cast a white mom and black dad with two kids—one Asian and one Mexican. We didn't realize how absurd it was until someone pointed it out after the production.

One time I showed up at the auditions for our school's production of *The Diary of Anne Frank*. Our drama teacher stared at me and said, "Why are you here?" I told him I was there to try out for the part of Anne Frank. It took me nearly six months to realize that what he was really asking was why I, an Asian person, was trying out for the role of a Jewish girl.

Maybe it was naive of me to show up for the audition. But if I could cast color-blind, why couldn't he? After all, it was high school drama! It was *make-believe*. If I could pretend to be Victoria from the Spice Girls, couldn't I pretend to be Anne Frank?

In my eyes, acting meant pretending, and if you were pretending, you could be anything you wanted to be! Why couldn't I play a black person? Or a white person? Why couldn't they play me? We could all be aliens, for goodness' sake! Why couldn't we just pick whoever was best for the role, regardless of what they looked like? I didn't get it.

Years later, when I'd surpassed a million subscribers on YouTube and had a few TV/film credits on my resume, I was up for the lead in a movie that I will call *Repeat*. I'd auditioned, gone through callbacks, met with the head of the production company, and lo and behold, I booked it. My first starring role. This was a huge step for me! I'd had supporting roles before, playing the best friend or colleague, but I'd never been the star in anything I wasn't creating myself. I told everyone: my friends, my family, people I worked with. I had booked it! I was a lead! I cried in my car on the way home from the meeting, singing pop songs at the top of my lungs.

A week later, when I was on a set for a short film I was directing, I got a call from my manager. The paperwork had come in, and they were now offering me the best friend role. Would I take it?

Wait, what?

Hold up.

Why?

My manager had no idea. He said it came out of nowhere. Was I sure that the meeting had gone well? Yes, I was absolutely sure. They'd expressed so much delight that I was going to work with them. We'd even talked about the role at length, and what we each loved about the character and the movie. We'd left shaking hands, smiling, and excited for production.

Finally, I asked, very softly, very tentatively, "Is it because I'm Asian?"

My manager was quiet on the other line. After a moment, he said, full of confusion, "Honestly . . . I thought that too. What else could it be?"

We got off the phone. He promised to call me when he had more information. I cried. I was Asian when I auditioned. I was Asian when I went into callbacks. I was Asian when I was in the room talking to them, shaking their hands, looking at their faces. I still am Asian. I'm always going to be Asian.

Why would they give me the role and then take it away? Could it really be for something as simple as the color of my skin?

My manager and I decided to pass on the best friend role. *Repeat* came back and asked that I take it. They'd cast the lead with a star; surely I could understand. Yes, she was Caucasian, but she was an experienced actor with a brand name. Although I can't argue with the logic of casting a bigger star to sell your movie, I still felt bitter that the role I had initially been offered ultimately went to a white actress.

Eventually, after a lot of negotiating and talking to the director (who I loved and really wanted to work with), I decided to take on the best friend role. Two weeks before we were supposed to start filming, our Star Name walked away from the project. It fell apart. The director tried to pitch me as the lead so the production could go on—after all, they had given it to me once before—but the company couldn't be convinced. The project died.

This whole experience scared me. Before this point, I had always assumed that the role went to the most talented actor. When I saw white actors being cast in shows I'd auditioned for, I'd shrug it off, assuming the girl was a better actress than me and she'd won the role fair and square. I would audition for parts that were specifically written as

Asian in the script, and even those roles would end up going to white actors. I figured she probably brought that character to life in ways that no one else did. She probably WAS that character.

I've been in casting rooms before. I know what it's like to find someone who just IS that person or has that look. I wanted to give casting directors and producers the benefit of the doubt. Surely you wouldn't cast someone just because of their *race*.

And don't get me wrong. Token roles are just as bad as no roles. I've gone out for more hypersexualized Asian women and geeky best friends than I'd like.

But there comes a time when every person of color in the entertainment industry has to ask themselves: Is my race going to limit my career?

There are parts I will never be able to play. I will never, for example, star in a period piece set in the Victorian era. I want to dress up in one of those petticoats, dammit. Have you ever seen one on an Asian? No! And if we ever were to be cast in one of those movies, we'd probably play a servant or a railroad worker or a sex geisha or a mail-order bride or something.

Now I look at the casts of TV shows and movies and I take note when there's not a single person of color on-screen. I look at stereotypical, two-dimensional characters onscreen with resentment and *rage*.

I obsess over the projects Jennifer Lawrence and Amy Schumer and Amy Poehler are in . . . and then I feel a twinge of sadness. Where's the Asian one? Where's the Indian one? Where's the Latin one? Why are all the It girls white girls?

Sometimes I wish that I was white so badly and so earnestly that I cry. I obsess over the fact that I never have the same opportunities to do juicy roles like Brie Larson in *Room* or JLaw in *Winter's Bone*. I'm saddened by the fact that I always imagine white people as the characters in the stories I read, unless a specific race is stated in the text or revealed in the name. I'm depressed by the fact that the only role models I had growing up were Lucy Liu and Mulan, and both were best known for their martial arts skills.

I've been forced to confront the very real, very scary possibility that maybe, just maybe, the way I look is going to get in the way of—and limit—what I want to do. And that's a horrible fucking feeling. That's a damaging, insane thought. The idea that there is a ceiling, a barrier, or a *wall* in the form of the color of my skin fills me with such unspeakable anger that I don't know what to do with myself.

Then there are moments where you have to say no to roles *because* of your race. I booked a guest star spot on a TV show and ended up turning it down. My agent was pissed. I understood—she has to protect her relationships. But I couldn't bring myself to do it. I'd gotten the audition while I was in New York. I should have read the material before confirming my attendance, but my agent loved the show and I trusted her opinion. We hadn't been working together for very long at this point, so it was definitely my fault for not warning her about my boundaries. I don't do anything I can't show Dad; that's my rule. Don't get me wrong, I'll totally do a sex scene with Chris Pratt, but in that case my *dad* would be the one walking out of the theater. I'd proudly sit with him at the screening, shouting, "DAD! LOOK! THAT'S CHRIS PRATT! OMG!" It's his choice whether or not to actually watch it.

I was on the way to the audition, reading the sides, when I had a horrible realization. The guest star role was for a stereotypical hypersexualized Japanese girl. In the first scene, all I'm doing is making out with one of the douchey guys. In the second scene, I'm basically giving him a hand job offscreen, but not discreetly. I hated the material instantly, but I knew it was too late to back out. Besides, I love auditioning. And I particularly love auditioning when I don't care about the role. Those auditions are always the most fun, but they are also the most dangerous because you are likely to book the role. When you don't care, you're loose and in the moment and do your best work. You're not trying so hard to be perfect. You let the magic happen.

I went in and did the role. I nailed it. I went big and silly, and because I didn't care, I was relaxed and funny. The casting director and associate *loved* me. They tentatively asked if I'd do a Japanese accent as well, just in case the role called for it, and I thought, Here we go. Since I spent four years overseas in Japan attending public school and learning the language, my accent was spot on. One of the characters I had crafted and performed in my improv group at Groundlings was Michiko, an earnest and enthusiastic foreign exchange student. She's a crowd-pleaser.

Actors like Aziz Ansari refuse to do accents. That's cool, that's their call, and I respect them for it. Why can't the person just be American? Why do they need an accent? I hear you, dude. Most of the accent-riddled characters on TV aren't even characters. They're stereotypes. They're cartoons.

I have a different attitude. It's not better, just different. Why do you have to hide a very important part of who you are because of how other people are going to see you? Does having an accent make you stupid or ignorant? No. Acting stupid or ignorant WITH an accent is offensive. Trying to be funny just because you HAVE an accent is offensive. A character with an accent is just . . . a character with an accent. An accent is like a piece of wardrobe. It's supposed to accentuate the character, not be the entire thing.

I've encountered a lot of comedians who won't joke about race. Some of them say, "I'll never do jokes about my race. It's cheap. And I don't want to become that comic who jokes about their ethnicity."

I love jokes about race. I think there's a tactful way to do them. I may not always hit a home run with them, but as with *any* category of joke—dating, sex, friendships, family, relationships—you're either relying on clichés or you're rising above them.

With all that said, my Japanese accent *kills*. Michiko is

the character I use whenever someone wants an accent. She's a person I can play *with* the accent. She's confident, fun, and engaging, and I've often used her in my videos when delivering sponsored messages, because she's loud and jovial.

So I did the accent. I didn't care. I played the hyper-sexualized hand-job-giving bartender in this audition and made her the best version of Michiko possible.

I booked the role. Of course.

I read the full script, and she had two other scenes in the episode. After the make-out and hand-job scenes, she reappears and lowers out of frame to give the guy a blow job. Raising the stakes! Heightening! Wowee, didn't see that coming. In her last scene, she shows up at the guy's house to move in. Because now that she's fulfilled her sex goddess duties to a man she's known for twenty-four hours, she has to complete the "crazy bitch" stereotype and assume that they are now in love.

I turned down the role.

As I said, my agent was disappointed. She likes the show, and she didn't want to jeopardize her relationship to the casting agency. But I don't regret my decision. I know I would've had fun on set, and I know that I would have been funny. But I couldn't in good conscience perpetuate a stereotype that I actively fight against. I didn't want to take that job and compromise my integrity.

Now, I totally understand when people have to take those jobs. After all, the first movie gig I ever booked was a scene where I was being taught how to drive by a racist.

The entire movie was riddled with horrible race jokes (written by white people) and perpetuated harmful stereotypes. But when I booked it, I took the job. It paid my rent for a month, and I don't regret it. Now that I have the luxury of choice, I can be more mindful of what roles I want to take part in. Not everyone has that opportunity, and I get that.

Will the color of my skin affect my career? Yes, of course it will. I can't deny that now. The whitewashing of Asian roles in entertainment (Emma Stone in *Aloha,* Scarlett Johansson in *Ghost in the Shell,* Tilda Swinton as the Ancient One in *Doctor Strange*) speaks volumes. But that only furthers my desire to inspire other Asian Americans to pursue their dreams in the creative industry, make conscious diverse choices in my own projects, and be a voice that stands up for my community.

I'm proud to be an Asian American woman. So much of who I am comes from the color of my skin: my values, my work ethic, my point of view. I don't know who I'd be without those things.

I used to tell myself that I would succeed *despite* my race. Now I know I'll succeed *because* of it.

It's Okay to Want to Be Beautiful as Long as It's *Your* Definition of Beauty

I grew up a tomboy with a strong aversion to makeup. I resisted learning how to apply makeup until I became an actor, and by then it was too late. The learning curve on that art form is steep. The number of products and steps is overwhelming. I've watched a million makeup tutorials, purchasing products and following guidelines, only to find out I'm not even using the right color foundation for my face. It took me six years and endless research to master the cat eye, which is why I have it in every photo. I say it's my signature look, but in all honesty, I just can't do anything else.

When you live in Los Angeles, you're surrounded by the most beautiful people in the world. I've worked on sets with eighteen-year-olds who are tall goddesses with big breasts and perky butts. I'll look up at their perfect faces and wistfully wonder why puberty is a cruel god who did nothing for me. I'm in my late twenties still playing flat-chested teenagers on TV. I've spent hours on celebrity gossip sites about stars who've had plastic surgery, looking for reassurance that no one could look that good naturally.

I used to get depressed about the way I looked. I'd see the leading ladies of the world and know that I would never look like them. I'd stalk celebrity Instagram accounts and try my best to mimic their style or makeup. But this only served to make me more unhappy because I didn't feel like myself. I felt like a hand-me-down version of someone else.

The pressure to be beautiful is enormous. Not only in the entertainment industry, but for all women. We're supposed to be beautiful, but we're not supposed to try too hard to look beautiful, or appreciate our own beauty, or we risk being called vain or shallow. It's impossible. You can't win. Either you're wearing too much makeup or you're not wearing enough. Either your outfit is trying too hard or you didn't even bother to try.

As someone who has been forced to edit my own videos, watch my stand-up performances, and sit through movies or TV shows I'm in to review my performance, I can honestly tell you: I know every flaw on my face. I know that my nostrils are different sizes and I have an up-turned nose. The left side of my face is stronger than my right, so my smiles are often crooked. My upper lip muscle, for some reason, is so strong that it curls my lip inward when I'm smiling genuinely, showing off all my gums. My eyebrows are distant cousins. I have to consciously hold my eyes open to make them "look alive" on camera (a note I've received often from directors and publicists).

But I know what my best features are too: My skin is flawless. My cheekbones are high, and every makeup artist I've sat in front of compliments my bone structure. I can make almost any hair length and hairline part work. Bangs or no bangs, I'm solid.

In 2014, I made a video called *How to Put On Your Face*. It was a satirical makeup tutorial that focused on inner beauty. As I put on eye shadow, I talked about viewing the world with optimism. I'd apply my lipstick and remind viewers to speak kindly. I'd had the idea for a long time, but I'd always thought it was dumb. But then I had a week where I was feeling particularly depressed about my appearance and I decided to just do it. I wanted to reinforce the idea that the inside matters as much as the outside, and somehow making a video with a lesson always helps me stick to my guns. There's a pressure to practice what you preach. And I didn't want to be a hypocrite—I wanted to follow my own example.

How to Put On Your Face went viral. It got picked up by the *Huffington Post* and Upworthy, and at nearly four million views, it's my most-viewed video to date. It reached people. It spoke to women everywhere who were just as tired of hating their faces as I was. Women are taught to place so much value on the way they look. We tell young girls that they look cute or pretty instead of telling them they're funny and smart. And pretty privilege is real. On days when I dressed up at my waitressing gig, I would receive twice the amount of tips as on the days when I didn't. Beautiful people are given more attention, more leniency, more compliments, more *everything*. With the whole world judging the way a woman looks, it's no wonder we judge ourselves just as harshly.

A few years ago, there was a huge controversy online about whether or not makeup guru Michelle Phan had gotten a chin implant. From looking at photos, it was obvious that something had been done. Though Michelle got some push back from fans who were angry about these enhancements, I thought she looked good. Her chin had always been her weakest feature (something she said, not me) and I'm sure it gave her quite a bit of anxiety. Being in the public eye means everyone and anyone feels that they have the right to comment on your appearance. Women are particularly prone to criticism of their face and body. And trust me: the constant criticism gets to you. Especially if you agree with it.

Seeing the backlash Michelle (and many other women) received for getting cosmetic enhancements and given the success of *How to Put On Your Face,* I was nervous about going there. But another part of me was curious. I'd wanted lip fillers long before the Kylie Jenner trend started. I hated how my top lip curled inward when I smiled. I'm sure no one else notices it, but it bothered me. It made me feel self-conscious every time I laughed or smiled. I kept trying to control it in photos or on camera, which would look strange and forced.

So finally I said, fuck it. I'm gonna try it. There's a lot of shame and stigma surrounding the idea of cosmetic enhancements, but ultimately I'm not ashamed of my decision because I did it for *me*. I love it. It's subtle, and only a few people have even asked me about it. My friends and family say it's not even noticeable. But when I smile, I have 50 percent less top gum showing. For me, that's success. I can laugh freely without covering up my mouth with my hand or actively trying to keep my lip down. I'm no longer wasting time with facial exercises to strengthen my lip muscles. I no longer feel insecure.

More important, I feel more beautiful. And that's okay. It's okay to want to feel beautiful, as long as it's *your* definition of beauty. I want to look my best so I can *feel* my best.

I want to be clear: I'm not saying lip fillers or plastic surgery is something everyone should get. I'm not saying give in to your every insecurity. I thought long and hard about whether or not it was something I wanted to do, if I was doing it for the right reasons, and if it was worth the money (it's a lot of money for just a slightly better smile). I did it for the same reason I got braces. The same reason I use moisturizer every night. I want to take care of myself to the best of my ability, inside *and* out. Will I ever do it again? Probably not. Five hundred dollars is a lot of money to pay for a slightly better smile. But I'm glad I tried it. There's no harm in figuring out what makes you feel best.

The best beauty advice I ever got was "Enhance your

strengths. Tweak the weaknesses." Beauty isn't about trying to look like someone else—the new It girl or the model who is having her turn in the spotlight. Beauty is not about conforming. It's about making yourself feel good and confident, and there's nothing wrong with that. People will judge us no matter what—if we get plastic surgery, if we're too skinny or too fat, if we wear too much makeup or not enough. It's important to figure out what matters to you and make choices that will make YOU feel good. Beauty is in the eye of the beholder, but the only beholder that matters is you.

You Can't Treat
an Emotional Problem
Physically

—

've been stick thin for most of my life. Before I started doing aerial arts and weight training and gaining muscle, friends and family would ask me with genuine concern if I had an eating disorder. I heard it all: eat a sandwich, put some meat on your bones, guys like girls they can grab, and on and on. It took me a long time to admit that maybe my relationship to food wasn't healthy, but not for the reasons people thought.

I was a binge eater. I'd eat until it physically hurt. I'd eat even when I wasn't hungry. Anytime there was food nearby, I was eating it. I'd stuff snacks into my purse and take other people's leftovers home. I'd accompany my mom to the grocery store, pick out my favorite items, then stash them in my room once we'd gotten home.

I loved the sensation of eating, the taste of food, the feeling of it in my stomach filling me up (until it's too late and too much). I'm not sure why I did this. Maybe it's because my parents always told me to finish everything on my plate. Maybe it's from the ROTC camps I went to as a kid where I'd be physically exhausted every day and only given fifteen minutes to wolf down my food. Maybe it's simply because I *love* food. I live for it. I wake up every day looking forward to what I'm going to eat.

When I was in my late teens, my relationship to food was so unhealthy that when I was broke, I would still go to expensive restaurants by myself and max out my credit cards on $300 meals. Life's too short to eat terribly, I'd rationalize. Food is an experience that I'm willing to pay good money for! It keeps me alive. When I couldn't afford good food, I would binge on Costco mac and cheese, potato chips, and other junk food.

I also worked at a sushi restaurant. Because I could speak Japanese to the chefs and Spanish to the kitchen guys, I was a favorite of theirs and I'd often drop hints about how much I loved certain dishes. They'd happily cook something for me, and I'd spend all day stuffing my face with crispy rice and baked salmon rolls. When my shift was over, I'd put in a to-go order large enough to feed a small family and inhale it all at home. By then it was dinnertime, and I'd be off to try a new restaurant.

I denied my binge-eating habit for a long time. I wasn't fat, so it wasn't a disorder, right? Plus I rarely threw up. Sure, I would crumple up in a ball after a meal, holding my stomach in pain, waiting to slowly digest everything.

But that wasn't a problem as long as I was willing to sit with the pain and shame, right?

There was also the fact that my best friend ate just as much as I did. I used to joke that we both probably had tapeworms. We *loved* food and we could eat *so much* of it. Part of me romanticized the idea that two little Asian girls could eat as much as we did. Maybe eventually we'd be competitors in eating tournaments and put our skills to good use. I liked the disbelieving looks we received when we finished our plates and asked our dining companions if they were going to finish theirs. I felt oddly proud.

Then I started having serious stomach problems. Sharp stabs of pain would come from nowhere, paralyzing me for an hour or two at a time. At first it would only happen once a week or so, but soon it was happening almost every other day. I had no health insurance at the time, so the only doctor's visit I could afford was the Internet. I tried drinking ginger teas and cayenne pepper–lemon juice shots, but those only made my stomach problems worse.

On top of this, my financial situation was getting out of hand: the majority of my credit cards were maxed out from taking myself out to restaurants. I'd be late on rent, but I refused to cut back on food. It was out of the question. I could *die* tomorrow. Did I really want my last meal to be mediocre and bland?

Then I went to a seven-day silent meditation retreat in Joshua Tree. Initially I'd been convinced by my then-boyfriend to attend. He thought it would be good for me.

He dropped out at the last second, and since I'd already paid (a donation amount, but still), I decided to go anyway.

The retreat provided vegetarian meals for all seven days. I spent nearly every day waiting for when we could get food. I'd sometimes duck out of walking meditation and check in on the cafeteria, hoping for a snack. The spread was weak: apples, bananas, and almond butter.

On the retreat, I felt like I was starving. I wasn't, of course, but when you're used to being filled to the brim, anything else feels hollow and empty. I'd sometimes *run* to the cafeteria ten minutes before lunch started so I could be first in line. I'd wolf down my food, then discreetly step back in line to get a second helping. Occasionally a third. During the long days of the retreat, food was my salvation. Like it always was.

Though there was no talking among the attendees at the retreat, the instructors held daily lectures. On the fifth day, our lecture was on food. I was a little surprised. We'd spent the other days on more substantive topics: A teacher talked about his former drug addiction and how he found himself through meditation. Another discussed how childhood trauma determines a lot about how we view the world as adults. And there was one particularly moving speech from someone who'd had a near-death experience. Mindful eating? How underwhelming.

But as I listened to this instructor speak, I grew afraid. It was like he was talking right to me. He told the crowd how he was a binge eater. How he'd been skinny his whole life, so he'd never thought it was a problem. He talked about craving food the moment he woke up, and having an insatiable hunger that was only satisfied when it turned into self-disgust and physical pain. He was describing me. He was describing my problem. A problem I refused to recognize as one because the effects were invisible. Because who cares that a skinny person eats a lot?

I listened attentively to the rest of his speech. He encouraged everyone to eat their next meal mindfully. To chew slowly and relish each bite instead of inhaling their food. To breathe between bites and be grateful that you have food at all. To stop when you were comfortably full. That was the hardest thing for him to learn, he said—to stop when he was full.

We broke for lunch, and I didn't power-walk to the front of the line. Instead, I told myself I was going to take my time. Though my reflex was to pile food high on my plate, I restrained myself, aiming for a portion that seemed right for my body size. I sat down and forced myself to take small bites. I chewed thoroughly. I drank water and breathed between bites. I slowed down and ate mindfully.

I ate the whole meal and waited for the feeling of fullness to come. I felt a dull weight in my stomach, but nothing close to the fullness I was used to. I glanced at the line. There were still twenty or so people in it. I could go back up and get another helping. Maybe just a small one. A half one. I didn't have to get another *full* meal. I just needed to be *full*.

That's when I realized I did have a problem with food.

I craved the feeling of needing to get back up, of having to get more food. I was using food as a drug. I couldn't control myself. Worse, it was an invisible problem. No one else could point it out because it was something that no one else saw. Only I really knew how I felt about food, how much pain my body was in after meals, and how desperately I needed to feed myself physically to feel emotionally satisfied.

Over the next few years, my attempt at mindful eating had its ups and downs. It was particularly hard whenever I went through an emotionally stressful time like a breakup or a career blow. Though I've vowed to cook more, I am still prone to immediately say "Let's celebrate by going out to eat!" whenever something good happens, instantly thinking of all the restaurants and all-you-can-eat Korean BBQ places in town.

I'd often go to the other extreme—I would skip meals when I felt like I'd had too much for the day. This was a horrible idea. I'd just end up starving and then I'd binge again. My stomach grew and shrank, causing me pain and discomfort every time I ate.

Even though I'm now aware of my problem with food, I still love it. I grew up on steak and potatoes in a family that always encouraged second helpings. My father told me that the best things money can buy are good food and memorable experiences. My mother loved cooking huge portions, and we showed our love for her by eating everything on our plate. Food is still one of the things I am willing to pay good money for. Nothing makes me happier than trying a new Peruvian tapas place or introducing a friend to my favorite dish.

But knowing that I have this problem—and treating it seriously—helps me manage it. I no longer flippantly tell myself that it's fine because I'm skinny or because I don't throw up. I eat smaller portions. I drink more water between bites. I *breathe* and *slow the hell down*. Because my relationship to food isn't just about loving to eat. It's an insatiable, emotional craving. Filling myself up physically is just a way for me to temporarily feel okay emotionally. I'm trying to literally fill the void of emptiness. But just because my problem is invisible doesn't mean I should ignore it. If anything, it's an even stronger reminder to own up to it and be mindful about how I treat it.

———

Knowing yourself is the first step toward loving yourself. Embracing the flawed parts of who you are can only make you stronger. I know it sounds New Age-y and clichéd, but honestly, all I want is to be a better person. And I can only achieve that by realizing where I am now.

3

MONEY, WORK, AND CAREER

My job didn't exist five years ago. I'm living in the Wild West of new media. Who knows if it's here to stay? If I'm here to stay? Whatever happens, I've learned a lot about creating a career for yourself. Whether you're drowning in debt, trying to find a job you actually are excited to do, or are afraid of being your own boss, the following chapters are filled with the things I wish I'd known when I was starting out.

More Money,
More Independence

—

As a kid, I thought I knew what money did: you gave it to people and you got stuff in return. It was easy. It was simple. Money was what made life fun. There were so many things to want to use it for—candy, books, clothes. When you get older, though, you realize that it's not quite as simple. When you are an adult, you realize money is meant for bigger things—a house, a retirement fund, a safety net in case you have an unstable, brand-new job creating YouTube videos.

When you're in high school, no one ever really talks about how money works: how to make it, how to manage it, where to put it so it makes more money for you. My mom and dad never taught us jack about personal finance. I've probably Googled the difference between a Roth and a traditional IRA several dozen times, because when you don't learn it young, you learn it hard. And man, have I learned money *hard*.

I can't tell you how *you* should make money, but I promise there are a million ways to do it. Trust me, I've tried a lot of them, and I haven't even scratched the surface. I've always been interested in business. And my first venture was not unique—it was a lemonade stand. Now, quick sidebar here: I want to let you know that a lot of the business strategies I had as a child were—how should I say this?—dick moves. I didn't know anything about business. I was just a greedy child. I don't operate like that today. I discovered a little thing called ethics. But back to the lemonade stand.

I diluted the lemonade with water. I realized I could sell adults a really watery-ass cup of lemonade and make more money with my lemons and sugar that way. Pretty stupid, considering that the lemons and sugar were taken from my parents, so I had no overhead costs *at all,* but my head was in the right place. My heart, however, had no idea this was a mean thing to do to a nice adult trying to help out my "business."

When my lemonade stand went bust, as lemonade stands inevitably do, I tried selling flower seeds. By selling, I mean spending hours picking seeds from flowers in my neighbor's garden and then selling them back to her. When I told my dad what I had been doing, he burst out laughing. I had spent an entire day earning a $1 paycheck, but ultimately I had sold our neighbor's garden right back to her.

I didn't stop there. When I was in middle school, there was a girl who sold candy out of her backpack. I bought candy from her a few times until I thought, Hey, everyone loves candy! I should try this. The next time my parents went to Costco, I insisted I come along. After I explained my business plan to them, Mom loaned me the start-up cash: $20.

I purchased the candy in bulk and used up all of my mom's plastic sandwich bags to package the product. I spent a few hours packing bag after bag after bag, then sorting them in the various pockets of my backpack. (After discovering all her sandwich bags were gone, Mom demanded I buy my own on our next Costco trip.) The next day, I opened up shop (my backpack) at the opposite end of the school from my rival. Thanks to Costco's bulk sales, I could afford to sell it at a lower rate, and I found people were pleasantly surprised to learn that my candy was *much* cheaper than my competitor's. Once I had most of the kids in the school getting their Skittles and Sour Patch Kids from me, the other girl eventually stopped selling candy. So of course I jacked prices way up. At twelve, I had effectively created a monopoly on the candy industry.

Sure, there was only one other girl selling candy, and I used super-unethical business practices to undercut her and push her out—but, hey, pretty impressive for a kid who didn't know jack about business, right? And it wasn't as if I were trying to be cutthroat; there were times I'd give Kris or Will candy, or eat my own product, or use my profits to buy us all something nice. I just loved having money. Money was power. Money was magic. You could turn it into anything you wanted if you had enough. And the profits were insane! I was making twenty bucks a day, baby! I was rolling in the cash money so hard that I was ready to upgrade to premium product: Gushers. Fruit Roll-Ups. Fruit by the Foot. But those dreams were short-lived.

Unfortunately, the school shut me down. I didn't have a seller's permit, and therefore I was breaking the law. If only I had known how easy it was to sign up for a seller's permit, I definitely would have continued fighting for the right to sell candy. The prospect of legitimizing a business with something as adult as a government-issued permit didn't seem within my reach.

Still, I was hooked. This wasn't a lemonade stand, this wasn't flower seeds, this was *real business*. Twenty dollars a day? To twelve-year-old me, it might as well have been gold.

I started looking for other ways to get green. I was a straight-A student and I loved reading. I read something like seventy books a year in my younger days (Stephen King level, son! *Sweet Valley High* all the way), so I figured that I should try to turn my leisure hours into paying hours as well. My middle school had a program where we had to read books and take computer quizzes on the material for points. You needed a certain number of points in order to pass your grade, so I started offering my services. For a price, of course. Hand over your username, password, and GPA, and I'd make sure you passed. Though I didn't have the vocabulary for it then, I was charging people flat fees before I could fill out a W-9.

It was a hit. Soon people were asking if I did essays as well. Essays? You better believe that seventy-books-a-year little old me loved writing fucking essays. Essays were my bread and butter.

I was also pretty good at drawing. When we lived in Okinawa, my parents chose to live off the military base and enroll me in a Japanese elementary school. I learned the language and the culture, and one of my best friends, Sayaka Yonaha, taught me how to draw in the classic anime style. I'd spend all-nighters obsessed with getting the figures and postures just right. When we made the move to Hawaii, someone at school saw a drawing I was working on and said, "Hey! That's pretty bad." I was a little behind on slang, so I didn't realize that by "bad" he meant "good." So I yelled at him and said I'd like to see him do better. How dare he insult my art? What a jerk. He held up his hands and said in that old Hawaiian pidgin, "Eh, brah. I meant it was *good*. Bad as in *good,* brah. You should be charging people fo' yo' pictures, ah."

So that's exactly what I did. You make such a cute couple, I'd gush. Why not buy your girlfriend a cute Japanese drawing of the two of you? Buy your friend a homemade card instead of a dumb one from the store. Want a portrait of yourself? Here, I can *create* a selfie for you! You don't have to wait a week for the disposable prints (oh, the simple life before Instagram).

I started taking a closer look at all my hobbies—could

I make money from them? What other skills did I have? Painting, reading, writing, drawing. I wanted to make money off the things I'd always done for free.

But then puberty hit. I started to notice boys. My love for making money was replaced with my desire to be loved. I still had an online shop where I would sell my paintings and drawings, and I'd still write essays for people on occasion, but I stopped asking myself how I could make my passion into profit. I started chasing other things.

That was unfortunate, because my desire to *spend* money didn't stop. In high school, I picked up a few jobs. But they were just that: jobs. I worked as a DJ's assistant, hauling amps and equipment to and from school dances (why anyone would hire a scrawny fourteen-year-old girl to do this, to this day I do not know). I got a job at a smoothie place in the mall, babysat nights and weekends, and worked at various retail stores during the Christmas season. I was no longer an entrepreneurial businesswoman, I was a worker bee. I started seeing everything in terms of work hours. This sweater? Five hours of work. Not worth it. My phone bill? Two weeks of work?! Are you kidding? I did NOT text that much. Those shoes? Way too many hours of work—forget it.

Then another horrible thing befell my ignorant financial self: credit cards. No teen should be allowed to have a credit card until they've been thoroughly prepped on personal finance. Credit cards and impulsive spending are the reasons I ended up tens of thousands of dollars in debt. Credit cards allowed me to fuel what I only later realized was an extremely unhealthy addiction: collecting things. It was so easy to buy the mint first-edition collection of the *Watchmen* comics on a credit card. Plus, eBay made it a game, a competition, something you could *win*. I was a sucker for winning, especially if I won something rare. My logic was: If it's popular now, of course I should buy it! It'll only increase in value over the years! What an asset!

So wrong. So. Utterly. Wrong.

You see, my dad's obsession with collecting things had been passed down to me *hard*. I still have a strong memory of him purchasing entire packs of Pokémon cards that he would never open, in the hopes that they would appreciate. He'd collected comics too, *before* they were a thing. He had the first issues of Batman and Superman comics, stowed away safely in his garage, steadily earning their value for years until my grandmother gave them away to strangers. In many ways, the finance world was cruel to my dad.

Mom and Dad grew up in poor families and had never learned much about finance themselves. The only financial advice they ever gave me was, "You want it? Save up for it and buy it."

Not "Save up at least a year's worth of your expenses to cover yourself in the event of an emergency."

Not "Do not accumulate more credit card debt than you can pay off within a month."

Not "Here's the difference between a Roth and traditional IRA so that you never have to search for it online as an adult."

If I wanted something, I saved up for it and bought it. Credit cards? Credit cards were just the reverse of that, right? Buy it, then save up to pay it off! Like layaway, right? Just way more convenient.

By the time I was twenty-one, I was $20,000 in debt. This was also when I decided to move to Los Angeles and pursue comedy.

What a horrible idea! Move out of your parents' rent-free, food-filled home, just to be two hours away in the city. I bought my groceries (and food for my three cats) at the 99-cent store. My phone was shut down every other week. I often had to borrow rent money from Dad or Will. I had no idea how to pay off my debt, much less save up for an emergency or retirement.

I had so many weird Craigslist jobs in my first years of living in the city. I once got hired as a cocktail waitress, but when I showed up to work, I was ushered into a room with a bunch of other ladies. When a customer walked in, we had to line up in a dark hallway and say our name when a flashlight was put on our face. If the customer picked you, you hung out with him all night. There was no drinking allowed, but there was hand-holding if you wanted (I couldn't help but notice all the wedding rings on the men who wanted to hold hands). I made a video about it years later and someone told me it's called "hosting." It's apparently very popular in Japan and quite normal there. But here? In the sketchy, dirty streets of downtown LA? I lasted a day, despite the $18-an-hour wage and the minimum $100 tip per customer. It was just too creepy. The whole place felt like it was sucking my belief in love and humanity out of me. But kudos to the women who could flash a smile and pocket the cash. I had respect for them. That was some of the finest acting I'd ever seen.

Then there was the time I worked as a waitress and shoulder masseuse for an underground poker ring. I brought the guys alcohol, gave them shoulder massages when they asked, and offered them snacks. I'd been brought up playing poker and blackjack and it served me well when I was asked, one time, to sit at the table. Amused, my boss fronted me a grand and said if I won anything, I'd split it with him. Games (and shifts for us girls) could go on for twelve hours, sometimes days. I happily took the $1,000 worth of chips, sat at the table, and smiled and gabbed like a moron. They grinned and leered and flirted until I started taking all their money. I actually used a trick I learned from Kristina. She had always started a game by going all in on each hand, or at least consistently. We would all fold, bitterly glaring at her unturned cards, sure that they were duds but not willing to risk our money on it. Then when someone finally wanted to call her all-in bullshit, she got lucky. She was always lucky.

I went all in a few times with duds and the guys folded, smiling and nodding, thinking that this silly girl had no idea how to play the game. Ha! I'm not gonna lie, that was probably the most badass I've ever felt. They had no idea I'd been raised on Texas Hold 'em and craps as our Thanksgiving and Christmas go-to games. They didn't know Dad had taught me odds before we knew algebra. I turned my $1,000 into $5,000, split it with my boss, and was told I could never sit at the table again. Unhappy customers weren't good for business. I used the $2,500 I made to pay off a credit card, quit the job, and started looking for something normal. I didn't want to keep working jobs where I felt the need to text Dad my location with "If you don't hear from me in two hours, send the police."

Minimum wage is supposed to be a wage you can live on, but I could barely make enough to cover my expenses when I was working four jobs: chiropractor's assistant in the morning, waitress in the afternoon, babysitter in the evening, and an on-call personal assistant at all other times. And it still wasn't enough to get ahead. I was barely treading water in the financial ruin I had created for myself. If I hadn't eventually gotten into YouTube and amassed a following, there would be no way I could've survived living on my own.

My early twenties were riddled with fear: fear of not having enough money, of not being able to pay bills, of not being able to take care of my cats. So I did what I always do when I'm stressed—I read every book I could find on the topic of my stress. I would go to the public library and pore over *Rich Dad, Poor Dad* and *Personal Finance for Dummies*. I scoured the Internet for personal stories of how people overcame their debt or managed their money. I learned a lot from those books. I learned that, first, I should save up $1,000 in case of emergencies. No matter what, I was to put 20 percent (or whatever was realistic for my financial situation) of every paycheck into savings until that number hit $1,000. Then I was to attack my debt. I had to put 20 percent (or, again, what was realistic) toward my debt, targeting the smallest amount of debt first. This way, victory would come quicker. Once I paid off my smaller debt, I'd *feel* better. You don't want to tackle the huge debt and never feel like you're getting anywhere. Tackle the smallest amount first. Give yourself a win.

Next, you're supposed to tackle the debt that has the highest interest rate. Interest rates can kill you. You could be making minimum payments for the rest of your life, but the damn interest makes those payments mean less than the amount they are. Kill the highest interest rate, kill the biggest thing working against you.

After that, keep attacking your debt. If you were hit with an emergency situation (which I was all the time—I had a damn VW Bug that was always breaking down), go back to building up the $1,000 till you hit the mark, then return to attacking the debt.

Once I put this financial plan into place, things were fine. Slow, but fine. I'd book a commercial here or there that helped with the monthly expenses. I wasn't anywhere close to paying off all of my debt, but I did feel like I had some control over my life, and less stress because of it.

As my YouTube channel grew, so did my AdSense earnings (my share of the ad revenue earned on my videos). They were small payments at first—$200 a month or so. Over the next three years I had a few viral hits: *How to Put On Your Face,* a satirical inner-beauty makeup tutorial, got a ton of press attention and circulated across Facebook, and *I Won the Lottery,* a fantasy exploration piece on everyone's daydreams of winning big, was also hugely popular. I did a few collaborations with other prominent YouTubers that gave my subscribers a boost. After several years of making a video a week, I was finally making enough from YouTube to pay off my monthly bills.

As I passed the one-million-subscriber mark, brand deals started coming in. At first I resisted the idea of sponsorships. The reaction on YouTube to sponsors was widely negative at the time. People often called you a sellout, accusing you of compromising your creative integrity for brand dollars.

But I was growing bored of the weekly videos. I was lonely. I was using a vacuum cleaner as my stand-in, running my own lights and sound, and filming in my house alone. I felt isolated and creatively stuck. I wanted to do short films and direct a crew and interact with other people.

In 2014, I told my audience that I'd be taking in brand dollars on my weekly show, but that I'd be putting the money toward short films. Brand money was twice or three times as much as my monthly revenue, and I could put the sponsored messaging at the end of my videos so that anyone who didn't want to watch could click off. To help people with the transition, I made the ads as entertaining as possible: taking audience suggestions for accents or characters, and delivering the branded message as such.

And to my surprise, I loved the challenge of making sponsorships engaging and entertaining. I was hoping to make longer short films in 2015 (*Loose Ends* and *Supers &*

Associates), so I started investing almost as much time into my branded spots as I did the weekly videos. Using ad dollars, I bought a green screen and a new lighting kit, and I hired a graphic artist, an editor, an assistant, and a director of photography. I was no longer a one-woman show, and my content benefited from it.

In 2016, I realized I probably wouldn't have a YouTube career forever. I'd seen people come and go, the viral memes burning out quickly. I decided that I should do adult things like start a retirement plan and an IRA and buy a home. I still worked hard on making my advertisements entertaining, but I took a break from short films to focus on selling movies and series.

The best advice I ever received about money was from a friend's father who is now my CPA. David said, "You should only ever spend your money in two ways: One, if it's going to help you grow your business. And two, if it's going to make your life easier."

If I had to pass on this advice, I would add, "And food. Good food is fine too."

When it comes to money, I've done it all: I've hoarded every penny, building up my savings account, and I've splurged, maxing out every credit card. Like most things in life, the sweet spot exists somewhere between those two extremes.

Financial independence is a beautiful thing, and I'm grateful for it. It's something I won't ever take for granted. And for those of you struggling to get there, know that it's possible. Know that you can do it.

On Being an Internet Personality

I came of age alongside a hell of a beast: social media. We both reached our adulthood at the same time, ready to take on the world while it took over us. When I was growing up, everyone wanted to be a movie star or a musician. Nowadays, teenagers grow up wanting to be YouTubers, Snapchat stars, and social media personalities. Thirteen-year-olds are making six-figure brand deals. Our pets are Instagram models with millions of followers. The average baby plays videogames better than I can. For better or for worse, the Internet has changed us. I didn't have a cellphone till I was seventeen, and even then it was a piece-of-crap Nokia that had pixelated text and the snake game. I shudder to think if I'd been born five years later, just how many of my naked selfies would exist in this world? Too many. *Too many.* I thought I was such hot shit at sixteen.

I have a complicated relationship with the Internet. On

one hand, I love it. It allows me to look up anything I want to learn or know. What were these little red freckles on my face after I threw up? Oh, blood vessels that burst. Cool. Is it bad to stand with my face up next to the microwave? Definitely (I probably could've guessed that). I'm able to express my opinions through video or the written word and anyone can watch or read it. I have access to virtually anything and everything from the comfort of my own home. I can meet new people. It's an amazing tool.

On the other hand, it can be a frightening place full of misogyny, racism, and unbelievable stupidity.

Maybe even weirder than the Internet itself, though, is Internet fame. It's one big through-the-looking-glass experience. One minute I'll be at VidCon (a conference for online creators), surrounded by hundreds of people who want to take a selfie with me. The next, I'm doing an open mic in a bar where no one knows (or cares) who I am. I go from being nobody to somebody every time I hit record, and I'm not always sure how to feel about it. Some days I feel like I have such an important part to play—being a role model, speaking up for suicide prevention and against bullying, making people laugh. Other times I wonder what my place is and whether this career in front of my computer is a fluke or a passing phase. I love my job because it allows me to speak from the heart, but it's hard when your professional and personal identities are so intertwined.

That goes double for when you're dating someone. So

just imagine how confusing it got when I was in a very public romantic relationship with another digital influencer in 2012. Being in the public eye put a lot of strain on our relationship. Like most online couples, we did daily vlogs and joint business ventures, which at first was great. It was fun working together and coming up with interesting ideas that we could film and send out into the world. But what I wasn't prepared for was the amount of scrutiny we would get back from the world—or that *I* would get, I guess. From the comments on our posts, people seemed to assume that I was a gold digger, an idiot, not worthy of the guy I was dating. At times I felt like I couldn't be my own person, always referred to as "the girlfriend." As I grew my own YouTube following, some people implied that all of my success was due to him, and that the work I put into my own channel amounted to nothing. It got hard to face the comments. After you hear something enough times, you start to wonder if it's true. The fact that our relationship was public made the breakup so much worse. Even now, *years* later, I still get comments about my ex on all my social media platforms. As I write this, someone just tweeted me a photo of my ex with his new partner. Sometimes it really does feel like it never ends.

Reading that last sentence reminds me that because I'm an Internet personality, everything I experience feels heightened, whether it's a relationship, an embarrassing photo, or a lighthearted joke being scrutinized. It's hard to remember that you're such a small part of the world. And all those numbers of views and likes and comments you can't comprehend onscreen? It's easy to forget that they're just people.

I think my biggest fear when it comes to online celebrity is letting it all go to my head. Falling into this trap of thinking I matter. Do you know how many channels get one million views per video? Over thirty-seven thousand. Yup.

Plus, what do likes, subscribers, and followers amount to in the end? I don't want to measure my self-worth with an algorithm. My self-worth is measured by the stuff that *actually* matters. So much of that is unquantifiable. What I do for the world. What I do for other people. How much I help.

But it's hard. Because it's fun to watch your numbers climb on social media platforms. I rationalize the hours I spend poring over analytics as research. I tell myself that selfies are vital to expanding my Instagram following. I get wrapped up in reading comments, eager to hear what people think of me and what other topics I can cover that will appeal to the 1.6 million subscribers I've collected over the last six years.

And yes, some of these things *are* important to my job. But there's a fine line between analyzing data and being obsessed with it. Between creating assets for social media and being vain or craving validation. Between creating art and pandering.

For anyone who wants to become an Internet celebrity, my best advice is to remember that the Internet isn't technically real. I know that sounds obvious, but it's become *so* ingrained in our lives (the first thing I do in the morning is check my cellphone) that it's easy to ignore everything else in front of us.

It's easy to forget how valuable in-person experiences are. It's easy to sit in front of the computer screen and "interact" with the world. It's easy to go weeks without ever looking up from your phone, or leaving your house, or getting together with a group of friends.

Social media is a lie. It's what we want people to see. We curate our lives so that they look fabulous from the outside. We only show what we *want* to show. Sure, sometimes we want to show something vulnerable and true and honest, and those are beautiful moments. But for the most part? We're all holding up a mask of happiness and fun.

What you see on the Internet is part of me, but it's not *all* of me. I am not that articulate in real life. I am not that put together. Hell, I'm not even as smart as I come across on the Internet. I have so much time to think and write and revise and edit that what ends up onscreen is a perfectly polished essay. It's easy to forget that what we put online is a persona. An extension of ourselves. True in some ways, but ultimately false because we're presenting an image, not being ourselves.

Remember that the world we can see is the one that really matters, and never lose sight of that.

How to Be a Boss

Being a boss has not come easily to me. I'm a people-pleaser. I'm generous to a fault. I don't handle stress particularly well. I'm an excellent administrator, but managing people? Reprimanding them when things have gone wrong? Dealing with human error that has cost me money? Trying to be firm and fair without smiling and apologizing? I struggle with all these things.

I constantly remind myself to avoid emojis in business emails, saying "sorry" unnecessarily, and overeager exclamation points to prove my enthusiasm. I don't need any of these qualifiers. I'm a businesswoman! (I say this as I sit in my sweatpants with my cats underneath my desk. But I'll say it again: I AM A BUSINESSWOMAN.)

I still don't like certain aspects of the job. Telling people that I'm not going to continue working with them gives me anxiety dreams. I hate having to deal directly with corporations and companies that don't understand what I do, asking them to pay me more than they're willing. I'm constantly frustrated by numbers that I have no control over, on a platform that shifts its algorithm on a whim. But I know I have to deal with all these things because I've come to accept that I'm going to be a boss for a long time. The following chapters tell you what I've learned.

Give Yourself Permission

—

Being a figure of authority is hard enough as is, but when you look like a petite teenager, it requires some extra work to make people take you seriously. I've walked into meetings where people have assumed I'm the assistant, or where men in the room refuse to make eye contact with me (and it's not because they are shy or awkward; it's a deliberate power move).

I've been described as "bossy," "aggressive," and a "bitch" when I'm just doing my job. I've been judged in ways I know I wouldn't be if I were a dude. I've had people roll their eyes when I delegate tasks, mutter their doubt that I don't know what I'm doing, or straight up second-guess me in front of my employees. And these are people who get checks at the end of a workday, signed by me.

When you're the boss, you don't need anyone's permission. You have your own permission. Whenever I'm feeling unsure of myself, I look in the mirror and say, "You're a straight white man." It reminds me that as long as I am confident in who I am and what I'm doing, it doesn't matter what anyone thinks of me.

Don't apologize for your existence. Don't ask if it's okay. You're the boss. Do what you need to do to get shit done. Give yourself full permission to be confident in your choices, execute them without second-guessing yourself, and kick ass.

You Don't Need Balls

Being a female in a male-dominated industry has its challenges. I've pitched ideas, only to have a man pitch the exact same idea and get the credit. I've played parts that portray women as nothing more than an annoying accessory to a man. I've had people in power offer me their professional help in return for sexual favors.

It's a man's world and we're all living in it. For now.

I don't want to vilify men. There are lots of amazing guys in my personal and professional lives. Well-intentioned men who aren't aware that they're being sexist. Friends who simply don't understand because it's not something they pay attention to.

It's not your job to educate people about what it's like to be a woman in the workplace. Even if you're up for the task, you're often met with skepticism and disbelief.

When I've told my male friends about being dismissed because of my gender, they assume I'm making excuses.

I've met women who have internalized this misogyny. They believe there's only one spot for a woman at the table, and they're ready to fight you for it. I admit, I was once one of these women. I was jealous whenever a friend of mine succeeded. I was competitive about our accomplishments, and secretly rooted for her failure. If I lost a part to an Asian woman, I felt devastated. I was happier if it went to a white girl, because at least that made *sense*.

Then I directed my short film *Loose Ends* with an all-female crew. The vibe was calm, supportive, kind. We were three hours ahead of schedule every day. All of our cycles synced up, so we had tampons at the craft services table next to the bananas and chips. Conversations during lunch were about the various forms of sexism each of us had faced in the industry. It was the most comfortable set I'd ever been on.

I've embraced being a woman in this industry. Though I still give myself the ol' "you're a straight white man" pep talk whenever my confidence is waning or I'm second-guessing myself, I love the female characteristics I bring to my work. The thoughtfulness, compassion, social and emotional intelligence, and sensitivity I bring to set keeps my crew motivated and our twelve-hour days enjoyable.

There's a wonderful quote circulating on the Internet that I remind myself of often: "Why do people say 'grow some balls'? Balls are weak and sensitive. If you wanna be tough, grow a vagina. Those things can take a pounding."

Take Care of
Your People

Being a boss means being a leader. The best leaders take care of their people.

Most industries depend on teams of people coming together to meet a goal, create a project, or solve a problem. You're only as good as the person who cares the least. So it's important that everyone cares as much about the end product as you do.

Here are the rules I believe all good bosses should follow in order to create a productive and happy workplace:

- Compensate fairly and pay promptly.
- Feed people well and often.
- Show your appreciation verbally.
- Be clear and direct about your expectations.
- Know how to utilize the talents of those around you.

- Don't waste anyone's time.
- Be a pleasure to work with.

These things feel obvious, but sometimes we in the film industry get wrapped up in ourselves. We're so stressed out about deadlines and not going over budget that we forget we're all just humans trying our best to make this *thing*. We're all working toward the same goal. We all got into this business because at one point in our lives we watched a movie or a TV show or a piece of art and thought, I wanna make that. I wanna do that.

I've seen so many people get hurt on set because of the need to rush. I've had producers scream at crew members. I've been screamed at. There's so much bad behavior excused by the film industry because "the show must go on." No, it doesn't. It doesn't have to go on. The crew could completely walk away from a set. The actors could quit. The producers could pull the plug.

The show *can* go on, but remember it's just that: a show.

Crunch the Numbers

—

Being the boss has its ups and downs. On one hand, you have full creative control. You call all the shots. Things are done the way you want them to be (or at least you hope they are). It's your face on the screen, it's your name in the credits, all the glory is yours.

On the other hand, if anyone fucks up, it's on you.

Back when I was doing background for television shows, I knew a girl named Macy. Macy was *sharp*. She liked to buy duplex properties and condos and lease them to people. She was all about that real estate. She was confident that purchasing property in Los Angeles and having someone else pay the mortgage was the smartest way of doing business. She kicked ass.

Macy liked me. I was good at making people laugh, and we had a weird inside joke where we'd just say "dogs" in old-lady voices (don't ask). Macy was older than me and appealed to the part of me that was desperately seeking mentors. I asked her what her single most useful piece of business advice was, and she said with no hesitation, "Always, *always* crunch the numbers."

Macy believed in doing all of her own bookkeeping. She'd never had an accountant because she said that even your accountant—*especially* your accountant—could run off with your money.

This advice has come in handy throughout my life. When I started running my own shoots, I had a detailed budget sheet and I took great care to balance my checkbook. I wanted to be like Macy. I wanted to know how much money I had and where it was going, down to the cent.

It's because of her advice that I knew one of the people involved in *Riley Rewind* had mismanaged $13,000 of the funds he was given. He had no receipts. He had continually promised to deliver a budget sheet once production was over, but once we wrapped he admitted he'd never kept a budget sheet at all. It was a nightmare.

I tried retroactively creating a budget sheet myself, but even after I had accounted for cast, crew, equipment, locations, insurance, craft, and catering, I was still missing upward of $13,000. It had disappeared.

I no longer trusted this person, but he was in my friend group and continued to work with people around me. When a friend hired him to produce her show, I was conflicted. On one hand, I wish someone had warned me about his terrible budgeting before I hired him. On the other hand, I didn't want to be seen as talking shit.

Finally I decided to tell her about my experience with him and how his numbers had been off on my project. She looked into her own budget and found out that he'd been pocketing thousands of dollars every episode he produced, despite rarely being on set. She promptly fired him.

Financing is boring and tedious, but it will save you money. Always crunch the numbers.

Stand Up for Yourself;
No One Else
Is Going To

———

When I first started acting, I was so grateful to have a job that I never spoke up when I felt uncomfortable. When I was asked to perform stunts without a stunt coordinator present to ensure my safety, I said nothing. When I was soaking wet in an air-conditioned room with no warming jacket, I said nothing. When a director sent me into the bathroom three times to stuff my bra for a blockbuster movie, I said sure, okay, whatever makes you happy, sir.

A lot of actors I know have this same problem. We don't want to be seen as divas or demanding or hard to work with. We don't want to cause a fuss. I've been luckier than my friends: some have had to go to the hospital for injuries they didn't speak up about while filming, and others have fought legal battles with directors over whether or not nude footage of them could be used (don't listen when they say they won't use it; always get mutual approval in writing).

I quickly learned that I had to stand up for myself because no one else was going to. Ignore the voice in your head telling you that you're being annoying. Know that you're there to do a job, but no job should leave you injured, humiliated, or unreasonably uncomfortable. There are people in the entertainment industry who believe that you should "suffer for your art." They glorify the idea of an artist as a genius who is so broken and creative that they will stop at nothing to achieve success, no matter what the physical, mental, or emotional cost.

This is bullshit.

We do what we do because it's our dream, not a nightmare. It won't all be comfortable, of course. There are times when you have to push through crappy weather to get the shot, or hold an uncomfortable position for it to read on camera. There are times when we will all inevitably suffer for our art. But that should be the exception, not the rule.

Don't Sign Anything Unless You Understand What It Means

—

I've never felt more stupid than when a piece of paper *I signed* has screwed me over. In business, there will be plenty of people pressuring you to sign something, or people close to you assuring you that it's fine, or even lawyers giving you the okay. (Unless these lawyers are *your lawyers,* do not listen. And even then, read the document in its entirety.)

I first learned this lesson when a guy I was dating told me that lawyers were expensive and that I could use his. Uh, big mistake. We founded a company together, but no official paperwork was ever signed. His lawyer kept saying "We'll draft a deal for you two," but when there's no immediate money to be made, a lawyer is going to take all the time in the world.

We sold our first big project together to Netflix, and in

order to finalize the deal, paperwork needed to be signed. I had written the script, starred in it, produced it, and poured my heart and soul into this project that I believed in. I quickly skimmed the paperwork and wondered aloud if I should get a lawyer, but my boyfriend's assistant told me that they were in a rush to get this deal through. Plus his lawyer had okayed the paperwork. I hastily signed without reading it, assuming that my boyfriend had ensured that everything was in place.

Guess what? We broke up. Right in the middle of trying to get that project on TV. I was at a point where I could afford my own lawyer, and when my ex-boyfriend told me that I was to have no further role in the project, I dug up that old contract I'd signed. Turned out I wasn't taken care of like I'd thought. I'd basically signed away all my rights in exchange for $1. (A dollar that I was never even paid. Where's my hardest-earned dollar?) I'd given away all claims to the project, any creative say I had, and all of my involvement—acting, writing, producing—was compensated with one hundred cents.

My lawyer regretfully told me that I'd signed a very shitty contract. I was humiliated.

I wish that I'd only had to learn this lesson once. But I didn't, because that'd be too easy.

A year or so later, I was working with a reputable company that was trying to turn a short film of mine into a series. The head of the company was an older woman named Melanie who I had looked up to as a mentor and a role model. She was a ballbuster who was funny and clever and *got shit done*. I admired her and looked forward to working together.

Our deal had been with my lawyer for some time—four months, in fact. He assured me that their initial demands were a bit absurd. They weren't paying me much, but the contract stated that I couldn't work in film or TV or do any other Web series for the entire duration that we were working together. My lawyer said that this kind of exclusivity was usually only seen in television deals, where it could be a stipulation only because the company was offering a large amount of money to essentially hold someone for the project.

In my case, though, the company I was working with was offering no money and wanted everything. The digital landscape is all new territory. There are no standard deals or practices in place! It's how MCNs, or multi-channel networks, are able to ask for 30 percent of your revenue when a standard Hollywood agent and manager only get 10 percent.

One day when I was driving home, Melanie called me directly. She said, in so many words, that unless I signed the paperwork, they were going to *recast me in my own project*. She said, "I'm calling you because I have a relationship with you personally. I wanted to talk to you first."

I immediately called my manager (who, by the way, is the best person in the world). He was *livid*. This kind of direct call while a deal is being negotiated is *unheard of,* according to him. It was a threat. A bully move.

Wait, what? Melanie was bullying me? She wasn't just calling because she really liked me and wanted to give me a heads-up that the paperwork was taking too long? No, my manager said. She's probably made promises to the investors of the project, long before our deal was ever in place, and is now freaking out about time.

Despite my lawyer and manager being furious about Melanie's lack of professionalism, I caved. I signed the paperwork a little sooner than my lawyer would have liked.

As a businesswoman, I don't blame Melanie for what she did. I don't. She probably knew that if she'd called my lawyer or my manager with this threat, it wouldn't have worked. Her whole goal was to get me to sign. But I blame her for taking advantage of someone who respected and admired her. My lawyer wasn't being unreasonably slow; Melanie was the one offering unreasonable terms. Not only that, but shortly after my deal closed, they started using it as a template for all of their projects. They'd used me as a guinea pig for structuring future deals. No wonder it had taken so long to come to an agreement; they had no idea what they were doing.

I hope that I never, ever make these mistakes again. But this is new territory—not only for me but for tons of other people as well. All I know is that before I sign something, I make sure I read it.

Do Every Job

—

Most people who work as digital content creators are forced to do every job. We shoot, light, edit, act, direct, produce, market on social media, and God knows what else. We do it out of necessity—often because we start all alone, in our bedrooms, wanting to make stuff. And we don't have other people to help.

I'm an actor at heart, but every additional job I do makes me better at my craft. Editing made me realize that I have to cheat to camera (when you position your body and face toward the camera; it feels completely unnatural and weird but looks fine onscreen), otherwise you'll probably only see half of my face when I'm talking to a clone. Find your light; if you're not in the light, you're going to have to do the whole scene over. If you flub a line, just pause and redo it.

Being a director made me appreciate how little responsibility I have as an actor. As a director, you run the set. You're in charge of the story from start to finish. It's exhausting, and often all-consuming, so you learn to appreciate actors who stop goofing around when you're talking to them, who show up on time, who know their lines, who take direction, and who are attentive.

Working with the sound department taught me to hold on my lines if planes are overhead or a dog is barking. You just stop, wait till it's clear, then take your line back again. You don't put your hands where the mic is or else all they get is a giant pile of WHOOSH or the rustling of your clothing.

Gaffing was by far the hardest job I ever did because it was all manual labor. I carried heavy C-stands and clamped lights to those stands and lifted sandbags all over the place. Gaffing taught me more about directing, really. Know what shots you want. Don't waste people's time. Be as efficient as possible and the crew will love you for it.

Creating the schedule and being my own assistant director (the person on set who moves things along) taught me how to be efficient. Don't waste time getting more takes when you know you have it, or coverage you know you won't use (though the editor in me always wants more than we need). Keep things flowing so that actors aren't brought to set at 9:00 A.M. and not used until 5:00 P.M.

When you do every job, you understand what each department does, what they need, and how to best run a production so that things are efficient but still fun. Whatever field you're in, whatever industry you're hoping to break into, explore every part of it. Know it inside and out. Try out the jobs that no one wants, that everyone wants, that you didn't even know exist. You'll gain a world of knowledge, and it'll show.

Work Hard, Work Smart

—

I'm always surprised when I talk to someone or meet someone and they say, "I know you're so busy!" I don't know how people get this impression, but it's accurate. Beyond updating social media and putting out video content, a lot of my life is spent working on long-term projects in development, auditioning for things I don't book, and going to meetings that I hope lead to something.

I like that people see me as constantly busy. Working hard is something I intentionally set out to do. When I was first getting into show business, I knew I wasn't the most talented or attractive person trying to make it. You live in Los Angeles? You are forced to face *all* your insecurities. I'd meet six-foot-tall, drop-dead-gorgeous models who had the personalities to match. It felt so unfair. I was like this little troll with uneven eyebrows running around their legs and admiring their beauty *and* intelligence.

So I said to myself, there are a hundred thousand actors in Los Angeles and a lot of them are more talented than me. A lot of them are more attractive than me. A lot of them have the kind of charisma and attention-grabbing conversation skills that I can only drool over. But what I have, and what many other people don't, is a strong work ethic.

Though I often hated him for it, my dad instilled discipline in me from an early age, and it's one of the greatest gifts he ever gave me. Dad would pay me a penny per page that I read, or $10 per A that I earned, planting in me the idea that accomplishment equals reward.

But it's easy to work hard, especially if it's something your parents taught you. It's harder to work *smart*. When I was younger, I spent a lot of time working on projects that would ultimately go nowhere, or working on videos that I learned nothing from. I used to say yes to everything, because I didn't want to turn down an opportunity that might lead to another opportunity. I'm still bad at this, but I try a lot harder now to say no, especially to projects that don't really inspire anything in me. It's hard, because we all have bills to pay and cats to feed, but I'm working harder at working smarter.

Working smart also means not burning out. There's no point in pulling all-nighters to get a project done if you're just going through the motions. There's no point in working if you're not accomplishing anything. There's no point in making money if you're too busy to spend it on quality time and experiences.

Know how you work, then be smart about it and hit it hard.

Know Your Shit

—

I once worked with a young, up-and-coming director named Nancy. She asked if she could interview me. An easy shoot, she said. A few hours, tops. But those few hours ended up feeling like days. Nancy was hopelessly unsure of herself. She didn't know what she wanted to do or how she wanted to do it, and she was constantly asking everyone else on the crew what *they* thought. A simple interview that should have taken forty-five minutes at most ended up taking three hours.

I was a little pissed. Hadn't she done any planning for this shoot? Didn't she know exactly what she wanted?

Once we actually started rolling, Nancy wasn't great on camera. She kept fixing her hair, or stopping the take and holding up production as she mumbled to herself: "What should I ask? Did I already ask this? What do you think I should ask you, Anna?"

I didn't want to step on anyone's toes, but I also felt like Nancy was going to continue fumbling around and wasting my time unless I took the lead. She actually looked relieved when I pointed to an area that was quiet and bright and suggested we shoot there. I fed her questions before the camera rolled, told her how to cue me for my most interesting stories, and then got the hell out of there.

Nancy could be a great director. But I cringed every time she said "sorry." I cringed when she asked her cameraman for his opinion regarding her interview questions. I watched the crew grow more and more annoyed because Nancy, the director and leader of this production, didn't know her shit.

I've been guilty of not knowing my shit. I've been on conference calls where I'm supposed to be giving notes on a project I haven't had time to fully read and think about. I've been in meetings where I hadn't online-stalked the notable person I was with. I've ruined opportunities that way. You come across as ignorant, undeservingly entitled, and thoughtless.

So here's what I know now: always be prepared. Visualization gets a bad rap for being corny and New Age-y, but it works. It just means that you think about what you're gonna do before you do it. Put some thought into it. Know what you want. Be conscious of everyone's time.

Don't learn the hard way—know your shit.

If You Don't Know
How to Do Something,
Find Someone
Who Does

———

By 2014, my YouTube channel had become big enough that clothing companies were willing to send me clothing in exchange for promotion. Free clothes meant new outfits to put onscreen (you wouldn't believe how quickly you cycle through your wardrobe when you're playing all the characters in a video), and I happily accepted this swag . . . until I realized that I could be promoting my own swag. So I decided to create a clothing line called Ghost & Stars. It's something that has always been on my bucket list, and I'd saved up enough money by this time to start a new business venture.

I wanted Ghost & Stars to be taken seriously and to stand on its own, so I set out to find help from someone who had experience in clothing design and production. I wanted to locate someone who had already made all the mistakes and who I could learn from.

Maura ran a small company that made cute animal-inspired clothing. She did all the graphic design herself, and from what I could tell, the shop was pretty successful. She just kicked ass at illustrating cute pandas. It was perfect.

I offered her a consulting fee in exchange for teaching me how she ran her business. She showed me how, from start to finish, to make a garment. This saved me *so much time*. Of the $5,000 budget that I had to launch Ghost & Stars, $1,000 of it went to Maura.

Hiring her was worth every penny. She saved me hours that I would have spent researching various manufacturers, she taught me a quick and efficient fulfillment process, and she gave me a recommendation for a printing company that I still use today.

If you don't know how to do something, find someone who does. Locate people who are way better and smarter than you and learn from them. People are usually willing to share their knowledge for free, but that shit is power and you should be willing to pay for it (even if it's just a lunch or coffee). Thanks to Maura, I didn't have to waste time comparing reviews on which label printer would work best or which poly mailer could best withstand the wear and tear of shipping. I was able to focus on the designs and the creative work and create a product that I could be proud of.

Time is a thousand times more valuable than your money.

———

As much as being a boss can be a pain in the ass, I love my job. I love the freedom I have with creativity. I even love the responsibility, to an extent. It's given my life purpose when I had none. It's been the dream that I've been chasing since I was a kid. And I wish there were more badass boss women out here with me! So give yourself permission and get out here. Work hard and smart. Take over the world and inspire other people to do the same.

4

RELATION-
SHIPS

Nothing teaches you more about yourself than a broken heart. I've made a lot of mistakes trying to figure out how to have a strong, healthy relationship— with friends, with partners, and, most important, with myself. *A lot.* Here are just a few.

You Don't Realize
How Important Friends
Are Until You're
Friendless

Growing up, my family moved every few years, dragging me from one military base to the next, and so I learned how to make new friends easily. Each time we relocated, I was forced to start over as the new girl at school. I liked it. Every two years brought a fresh start and the chance to shape a new identity. I could be whoever I wanted. I'd try being the extrovert in Hawaii, the adventurous American in Japan, and studiously shy in Virginia. I could morph myself into whoever I wanted to be. It was fun. I was in charge of how people perceived me. And if I didn't like myself, fuck it. I would move in a few years and start all over again. I could try on different personalities and discard them at will.

Every military brat knows how to make friends quickly. You mirror body movements, mimic the way someone talks, shower them with (hopefully genuine) compliments, and try to find common ground. What do you like that I like too? How can I mold myself to complement your personality? How do I add a little yin to your existing yang? I think this skill has helped me as an actor. I'm used to slipping on whatever identity allows me to fit in best. I'm used to changing myself to suit the environment around me.

But my upbringing also had real consequences for me as an adult. I don't have an independent identity. I don't know how to maintain friendships because I've never had to do it. I have a distorted view of who I am. Whereas most people think it's dishonest to change yourself for the people in your life, it's the way I grew up. Even though it sounds dramatic, it's how I survived.

So when I moved to Los Angeles as an adult, I was excited about putting down roots somewhere. I couldn't wait to build a community and to stay in one place for more than a couple of years.

I've lived in LA for seven years now, longer than I've lived anywhere else. However, that hasn't meant that all of my friendships have lasted seven years. After some time spent in LA, I began to notice a pattern: I'd meet some cool people, become good friends with them, and then BAM—about two years in, I'd have a falling-out with that friend group and move on to another one. Each time it seemed like the same cycle on repeat. Instead of moving to another city, my best friend and I would get into a fight. We would go our separate ways. And I would be back out there again searching for new friends.

I asked my therapist if *I* was the problem. Why couldn't I keep friends? Was something wrong with me? By this point I'd been in therapy for years and understood my self-destructive habits. So was I secretly sabotaging all the good things in my life? Was this because of the way I'd grown up? Was I just reliving my upbringing by blowing up my life every two years to start again as someone new?

My therapist didn't think so. He pointed out that the reasons I usually split up with my friends were all justified, since I had a tendency to seek out emotionally abusive friendships. And that was true: The more someone took advantage of me, the more I wanted to please them. The more they took, the more I boundlessly gave. I'm still not sure exactly why this is. Does it come with the territory of being an attention-starved people-pleaser? Does rejection simply make me try harder? Only Freud could tell me, I guess.

And as much as I hate to say it, I don't have a best friend. Don't get me wrong, I desperately want one. I want someone to call when I have problems with my boyfriend. I want to have a go-to gal to get stoned with on the weekends so we can watch nineties movies and order more takeout than we can possibly eat. I want someone to shop and gossip with. Most of all, I just want someone I can call my own.

For the last three years or so, I've tried to find one. I'd

eagerly enroll in classes like aerial arts and improv, hoping to find someone that I would click with. I felt so pathetic as I talked to various women, desperately hoping that they'd like me and give me their number. It was like dating, but worse. I'm sure some women thought I *was* interested in dating. "Do you wanna grab dinner and a movie this week?" sounds an awful lot like a come-on instead of a plea for friendship.

One time I got drunk with an acquaintance of mine and we went back to her house to talk more. I noticed an uninstalled pole lying on her floor and offered to help her set it up. I stayed into the late hours of the night, drunkenly helping her assemble her new dance apparatus.

When I got home, I had a huge grin on my face. My boyfriend, who knew about my intense quest for friendship, asked how it went. I told him that I thought *this was it*! After all this searching, could this person be my person? I went to sleep happy and excited for what the future would bring. I had found The One.

We haven't hung out since.

At times I bitterly regretted my decision to drop out of college. So many friendships are formed in high school and college. Nothing can truly replicate the experience of being forced to hang out together every day, growing up together, making mistakes together, and having fun together all day every day. A lot of adults make new friendships through their offices or work, but I work from home.

Not only do I work from home, I'm also a workaholic with a self-imposed packed schedule. I take care of six cats. Most of the people I interact with on a daily basis are my employees (or cats), and a full-time friendship is hard to cultivate. It's an uneven power dynamic. Where can I go to find friends?

There were times I'd try to force a friendship on someone. I'd decide that they were going to be my new best friend, and I'd text and set up hangout sessions. It was fine. Hanging out was great until I realized that I was the only person ever reaching out. So I stopped reaching out, and never heard from the person again.

Then there were times that girls were eager to be friends with me. I was ecstatic. I didn't have to work so hard! They were hitting me up, inviting me to coffee or drinks, and I'd happily schedule a date and time for our friend date. But more often than not, these women had an agenda. They'd want me to promote something on social media or start up a YouTube channel with them (when I was already well established in the space and they had no experience whatsoever).

So here's my advice, whether, like me, you're still looking for that epic *Broad City* friendship, or you've just parted ways with a close friend, or you've just moved somewhere new. *You can't force friendship.* You can go looking for it, put yourself out there, and meet new people. But don't worry. It's something that will come naturally, over time, through shared experiences and circumstance. It's not going to happen right away. When it does, it may fall through. And that's okay.

Sometimes I feel like giving up on the pursuit of friendship. After all, a lot of effort goes into it: attending parties (I'm an introvert, and this drains my energy), inviting women out for coffee or brunch, asking if I can tag along with girls I admire. But female friendship is important. Even when I feel disappointed, that connection, however brief, is worth it. Each time, you learn something new about yourself and about relating to another person. I say this knowing just how utterly lonely it is to not have someone to confide in.

Maybe that's why my videos resonate with so many people on the Internet. They can probably feel my inherent loneliness! We can bond over our mutual sadness that we haven't found someone who makes us laugh so hard we can't breathe, or who will be honest when we're being bitchy. All I want is someone who loves animals as much as I do and who will get a drink with me even though it's ten in the morning. Even though I haven't found her (or him) yet, I will never stop looking. I'm also taking resumes and head shots from those who would like to apply.

Don't Be Afraid to Cross People Off the List

—

I have a tendency to stay in friendships that are toxic. The worse someone treats me, the more desperate I am to be liked by them. And I know I'm not the only one. There are a whole lot of people who fall into this exact same cycle. If someone continually brushes us off, the more we jump up and down shouting "Like me! I know I can make you like me if you give me a shot!"

Kristina's death gave me abandonment issues. I worried that if I fought with anyone and we left it on bad terms, they'd go kill themselves and I'd blame myself. As a result, I'm afraid to cut ties with people. I worry about upsetting anyone—friends, family, lovers, colleagues—even if they're detrimental to my life.

One of my best friends when I first moved to Los Angeles was a writer named Barbara. She'd seen a sketch I'd put up in a class showcase and wanted to work with me. I was ecstatic. After having done stand-up alone for so long, I was eager to collaborate with other people. I pitched a short sketch show to Barbara and we quickly became best friends. In both friendships and relationships, I am a giver. Whether it's compliments, gifts, time, or attention, I love showering a person with whatever I've got.

Barbara, on the other hand, was suspicious by nature. In college she'd been through multiple medical malpractice lawsuits, and as a result, she was paranoid that everyone wanted to screw her over. The more suspicious she became, the harder I worked to ease her fears.

I brought her on as a writer in a showcase I was doing for a network television show. I gave her my juicer after she offhandedly commented that she wanted one. I took on all the responsibilities for our sketch show—the editing, producing, marketing, finances. Barbara eventually brought me a contract. She had a lawyer friend she'd been talking to about our show, and she wanted it solidified in writing that we each owned half. I agreed, with the caveat that she take on some additional responsibilities. I asked her to take on budgeting and financials, since that was work she was qualified to do. She refused. She wanted me to sign the contract, but she wouldn't take on any extra work.

I reluctantly agreed, but that wasn't the end of it. Giving in to Barbara's fears had only made them stronger. Soon signing the contract wasn't enough. She was still convinced that I was screwing her over somehow. We'd have long fights on the phone where I insisted that my actions showed her how loyal I was. Why would I try to screw her over? She was my best friend.

"No, we're business partners first," she said. That broke my heart.

Barbara and I ended our relationship shortly after that. She had taken all I had left to give, and at that point, I realized that it would never be enough.

It often takes me a long time to recognize that I'm in a toxic relationship or friendship. But what I've finally learned is that when you do realize it, it's okay to cross that person off the list. It's okay to cut toxicity out of your life.

I don't think Barbara is a bad person. We've since talked and it's nice to hear that she's doing well. She apologized for her paranoia, and I understood and forgave her. If there's one thing I know, it's that we're all shaped by our past trauma. And in the few brief encounters we've had since our falling-out, I often ask myself if I should be friends with her again. It would be so easy to get brunch and catch up and continue making plans. It would be so easy to work together again. That old familiar feeling of nostalgia would creep in, and I'd imagine all the late nights we could have, working and hanging out and being best friends again. But ultimately, it's not worth having toxic relationships in your life. It would be fun for a while, but we'd fall back into our old patterns—her being suspicious and me eager to please. As much as I want more close friends in my life, I have to put myself first. I have to treat myself as if I were my own best friend.

Because if I don't treat myself well, why should anyone else?

Love

When I was little, my dream (besides acting) was to be a wife and mother. I was brainwashed by romance novels and fairy tales and movies and TV shows. I was addicted to infatuation. I had fantasies about walking down the aisle in a puffy white dress, seeing my belly bulge with life in the mirror, taking long walks on the beach with my husband, and blah blah blah. I'd lie in bed reading YA novels and imagining that someday my boyfriend would spoon me while I read. That's how selfishly I viewed love—I actually thought someone would hold me and do nothing for hours on end while I read a book.

Every time I went to the store or to a friend's house or walked the hallways of school, I kept an eye out for my *one true love*. My *soulmate*. The *One*. He was out there waiting for me, and he was perfect. All of his edges would fit mine and, like two jigsaw puzzle pieces, we would click neatly into place.

Ugh.

I've been a serial monogamist since I was fifteen. I've kept relationships going way longer than I should have. I'd build an epic narrative in my head about the relationship, and I'd be horribly let down when the person I was dating turned out to be just a human being. Not an immortal vampire with eternal love for me, or a fierce werewolf with a jealous streak and super strength, or a knight in shining armor who took one look at me and fell to one knee to propose.

In hindsight, I can see how crazy I was. I thought love was dramatic and high-stakes and fierce. After the honeymoon phase of a relationship ended, I'd become convinced that the lack of passion signaled that our love had ended. And sometimes, by that point, I realized there had never been any love there in the first place.

Once the relationship became more routine and mundane, I would begin to wonder: Am I not in love anymore? Is this how I want to spend the rest of my life? I'd notice all the little flaws in my partner, and instead of loving him anyway, I'd daydream for the golden days of yore. Where oh where had perfection gone?

We're taught to have unrealistic expectations about love. We expect our partners to be perfect, to read our minds, to put us above themselves. And we expect our emotions to always be strong and passionate, our relationships effortless, our happy endings predetermined.

For years, I spent most of my relationships in love with the idea of a person and what they represented, all while disliking the person I was actually with. I'd be attracted to the types of boys who would only mean misery for me—sex addicts, brooding guys with anger issues, ambitionless stoners—thinking that I, or love, could "fix" them.

I thought that love was synonymous with struggle. Every romantic movie and book I'd ever read was rich with conflict. The girl always cried and walked away, the boy was always moody or misunderstood. There were fights. If you're lucky, you fought (and made up) in the rain. These were the ideas I used to mold my own relationships. Misery meant it was working! Yelling at each other was the sign of *The Notebook*–level love!

It's only when I began going to therapy that I finally understood what healthy love was: communicating with each other, being clear and direct about your wants and needs, treating each other with respect, and trusting your partner to do his or her best.

It turns out that the best kind of love is quite boring. It's supporting each other on a daily basis. It's being in touch with yourself and knowing (and communicating) what you need. It's having realistic expectations for your partner, being responsible for your own happiness, and being a good friend. It's give-and-take. And it is *hard*. It takes work.

But before anyone bothered to explain this to me, I spent my teens and twenties in codependent, destructive, emotionally/verbally abusive relationships. I learned the hard way.

If He Doesn't Listen, Ditch Him

—

had my first serious boyfriend when I was fifteen. I was living in Hawaii and met Andrew at a friend's birthday party. He was a cute surfer who called me "ma'am," which I found insanely adorable. He was two years older than me, didn't take school seriously, and didn't really know what he wanted to do in the future. At the time I gave him a free pass on that one. I mean, we were teenagers, right? He was careless and reckless and impulsive—a free spirit, I thought. I'd happily do his homework whenever he asked me to "help," I'd write his essays when he insisted he had writer's block, and I'd cook him meals despite the fact that I hated cooking. It's easy to be a free spirit when someone else is doing everything for you for free, I guess. But being in love can turn you into an idiot, so I guess that made two of us.

Now, at fifteen your hormones are *raging*. I can't tell

you how many hours I wasted dry-humping him on the bench in front of our house. I could've taken a college course in that time. I could've read a dozen books. Instead, we dry-humped for about a year and a half and I ended up giving him my virginity for his birthday.

We were at his house in his bedroom. We weren't even alone. His family was home, but at this point we'd been dating long enough that they didn't care to check in on us. I remember thinking that this would be a huge moment. I wasn't going to be a virgin anymore. I was officially crossing the threshold of adulthood. I was going to be a woman.

I was nervous but, thanks to the Internet, I'd seen penises before. So no surprise there. When I was thirteen and we had dial-up, I'd look at porn and cringe with horror. Penises were so scary. They reminded me of the monsters from *Tremors*. They were veiny and weird and looked like faceless girthy men swaying back and forth. Even Andrew's penis freaked me out sometimes. I would hold it and it would be so *warm*. And he could make it twitch, which he often did because he liked my startled reaction.

But on the day I lost my virginity, I wasn't thinking about *Tremors*. Andrew slipped a condom on and laid me down on his bed. He kissed me and said he loved me and then I felt a rip. I'd read that some women liked it their first time, and that if you were a horseback rider chances were high that you'd already ripped your hymen open. I figured I'd done so many high kicks in martial arts that I'd probably gotten rid of mine a long time ago too. Nope.

It was so *uncomfortable*. It felt wrong, like he wasn't supposed to be there. The latex on the condom felt weird and Andrew's body on mine made it hard to breathe. It hurt so badly that we had to stop after a few minutes. I remember thinking that if just a penis could cause that much pain, I never even wanted to *think* about pushing a baby out of there. Forget that shit.

Luckily we'd had the foresight to lay down a towel, because there was a bit of blood. As Andrew cleaned it up, I sat there feeling nothing. I didn't feel like a woman at all. I didn't feel liberated or sexy. If anything, I felt like a kid who had made a horrible mistake. It wasn't the romantic moment that I saw in movies. It felt more like the porn I had seen on the Internet: rough and fake and filled with bodily fluids. Overall, it was disappointing. But I was happy that I'd shared my first time with someone I loved.

The second time we did it I felt a little better. By the fifth or sixth time, I genuinely enjoyed and looked forward to having sex. Though there were a few times I *thought* I'd climaxed, I definitely didn't. And I wouldn't for years, until I discovered clitoral stimulation toys. (But that's another book.)

Andrew and I would waste a lot of time watching TV, going to the beach, and playing videogames. But most of our time was spent thinking about, having, and looking for places to have sex. (Fun fact: Hawaii is known for having the highest pregnancy rate among teenagers. That's right. It's such a small island, you have nothing to do but each other.)

There was a girl in my high school—we'll call her

Arlene—who got pregnant twice. I saw her binge-drinking on the steps outside of school, and when I asked her why, she said it was "pregnancy control." It took me a few years to realize that she was trying to give herself a miscarriage. She got pregnant again her sophomore year, and her mom took her out of school for a few days, probably because she'd caught on to Arlene's form of "pregnancy control." She finally had a kid her senior year, and though I was living in California by this point, a friend told me it was because Arlene just knew "it was time." Seriously. And this wasn't *uncommon*. If I had to guess how many pregnant girls there were in my Hawaii high school, I'd say it was in the double digits.

Sidebar to the governmental powers who may be reading this: PLEASE make it mandatory to teach contraception, not abstinence, in high school sex ed classes. Don't you remember what it was like to be a teenager with throbbing genitals? Don't you remember how determined you were to find a suitable location for sex? Give teens condoms and the pill, not a lecture. Your words are falling on hot and bothered ears.

I think I knew Andrew and I were doomed a little over a year into the relationship. Andrew had a shiny red sports car that he'd just gotten for his birthday. It was used but looked cool. On this particular day, we were headed off to the beach. As my dad saw us off, he told Andrew to make sure to buckle up. He repeated it a few times and with grave sincerity. I thought this was super weird and rolled my eyes accordingly.

As we drove down the highway, I noticed Andrew's seatbelt wasn't buckled.

"Buckle up, babe," I told him.

"Nah."

I stared at him. "My dad told you to buckle up."

He shook his head. "Nothing's gonna happen."

"It'll take you like, what? Two seconds? My dad was all weird about it, so just do it."

Andrew looked at me. "Nothing's gonna—"

Of course, since the universe works in mysterious ways, he hit a car. His head flew into the windshield so hard he cracked the glass. His hand smashed into the dashboard and the skin split. His front bumper was dented and damaged.

I got whiplash, but it could've been worse. I was wearing my seatbelt.

Andrew was thankfully okay, but unfortunately, the insurance situation was not. Because he rear-ended someone, the fault was on him. His insurance only covered the other vehicle, not his own. The insurance investigators suspected he hadn't been wearing his seatbelt, and insisted this negligence meant they were not obligated to pay the medical bills he had accumulated for his head injury.

Since I was the only witness to the accident, Andrew begged me to sign a statement that said he had been wearing his seatbelt and that it must have somehow malfunctioned and released him upon impact, thus explaining the giant crack in the windshield and the giant crack in his head. He asked me to lie.

There was a lot that I would do for Andrew, a lot I *had* done. I'd do his homework. I'd clean his room. I'd fill his car with gas. I'd cook for him. I'd give him my love, my time, my body. I was in love, and like I said, love makes you a bumbling idiot.

But there was no way in hell I was going to lie on an official document when we'd argued about a seatbelt for two minutes and he'd said, "Nah."

All he'd had to do was listen. None of this would have happened if he'd listened to me or my dad. And not only had he refused, he asked me to lie. The more I thought about it, the angrier I became. He had put his life in danger. For what? To look cool or something? He certainly didn't look cool with the stitches on his forehead.

I put my foot down: I would not sign. Though he pleaded and fought with me about it, I didn't budge. He'd broken the law. He'd have to live with his mistakes.

I'm proud of this rare early moment of self-respect I displayed in my first relationship. It established where I wasn't willing to go. I knew it was unfair of him to ask me to deceive anyone on his behalf, especially when he had no one to blame but himself. My gut told me what the right thing to do was, and I listened.

Eventually he got over it. And then I got over him.

Take Your Birth Control

—

When I got pregnant I was young, broke, and dating this guy that we'll call Dick (yes?). I was twenty-one years old and had just moved to Los Angeles.

I met Dick while working on a TV show. I was a background artist (all the people you see in the background on TV and in films are hired extras) and I remember walking onto the giant studio lot and feeling awestruck. Hearing the strange lingo used on set was like hearing a language I hoped to speak fluently one day. I'd watch actors take their marks and directors call action (later I learned it's actually the AD who calls action on most big-budget productions), and I'd feel a sense of belonging and hope and excitement. It didn't matter that most people treated background like shit, or that our craft service consisted only of bananas and apples. I was elated. I had left the boring, soul-sucking classroom behind and walked right onto a living, breathing, *filming* set.

The day I met Dick, I was running late. I ran to the second second assistant director (they're in charge of all the background) and apologized for my tardiness. The second second, a tall guy with dark blond hair and killer blue-green eyes, said not to worry. He introduced himself as Dick and shook my hand. Though I immediately liked him, I never considered him a romantic possibility. He was tall, handsome, in his thirties. I wrote him off as out of my league. He probably dated models or whatever.

Later that day as I was signing out, Dick asked if I'd like to be on the show again. I loved working background when I could. You sat around all day until you were needed, so I often could spend the downtime working on writing sketches or stories—all while being paid. Plus there was free food. And in those days I was buying my groceries at the 99-cent store to supplement all the Costco mac-and-cheese packs my parents had bought me. I wanted all the free hot meals I could get.

Dick asked for my number so he could book me directly. I gave it to him, and sure enough, every week he called me for work. I loved it. When working background, you normally rotate between many different sets. But working on only one show gave me a chance to get to know the cast and crew. I developed friendships and professional relationships. The lighting guys happily answered all of my questions about setups and color temperatures and the basics of three-point lighting. I learned why sound people used both booms and lavs. A lot of my technical knowledge of filmmaking is from working (and asking endless questions) on that show for a year.

Dick was great to work with. As a background artist, you get used to people screaming at you and treating you like you are subhuman. Sometimes you're not given ample (or healthy) food or cover in harsh weather conditions when you're filming outside. It can be—and usually is— a nightmare. Dick was a refreshing boss. He was kind and friendly, and he treated everyone with respect. Everyone working background loved him.

One day, while signing out of work, Dick started to flirt with me. I was taken aback. I hadn't known this was on the table. But now, suddenly, all bets were off. If he was flirting, that meant he found me attractive. Since I found him attractive also, I could now relentlessly pursue him. It didn't take long till I was asking Dick when he'd take me to dinner, sending him smiley-faced emojis in my texts, and imagining what his butt looked like underneath those baggy cargo pants.

I was friends with another girl on set named Rachel. We bonded over how adorable we thought Dick was. I'd notice them flirting in a hallway, and instead of feeling jealous, I took it as a competition. May the best wooer win. The easygoing nature with which I pursued Dick changed when Rachel told me that Dick's brother had died a year ago.

My delusional self immediately created an entire romance novel starring us. Two survivors. It was a confirmation that we were meant to be together. We could understand each other's pain. We would help each other heal. In my head, we had an insanely deep connection that no one else could comprehend. We shared a mutual grief, an understanding of mortality and death.

I was an insane person. This is why they say don't date actors.

From that point on, I bugged Dick *a lot*. I'd text regularly: When are you gonna take me out? When are we gonna have dinner? Part of me liked the competition with Rachel (I would prove my love and beat my foe), and part of me was seriously buying the romantic narrative that I'd been feeding myself.

Finally Dick caved and took me out on a first date. He picked me up and we went to eat sushi in Venice. Over dinner I learned that he liked to meditate, was an aspiring director and an avid reader, loved the outdoors, and didn't believe in monogamy.

I asked him to elaborate on that last point.

He shrugged, saying that he thought it was an outdated concept that no man could uphold. I, like most hopelessly infatuated idiots, figured that he just hadn't met the right person yet. After all, he'd had girlfriends before, hadn't he? He said he'd once proposed to someone right after college, but she'd turned him down. That explained it! He was probably just afraid of getting hurt again. And I wouldn't hurt him. No, in fact, I would *heal him*. Our love was *that special*.

He dropped me off at home and gave me a fist bump. This mysterious gesture only fueled my attraction to him. I probably thought something stupid at the time, like: Wait till I tell our grandkids about this! Your grandpa dropped me off and gave me a fist bump. He liked to play hard to get.

Although I didn't have a ton of interaction on set with Dick because of his demanding job (and the fact that he wasn't supposed to date people he worked with), I got serious about wanting a relationship with him. One time I saw him flirting with Rachel, touching her shoulder and laughing with her. I got so pissed off I ran up to one of the other actors on set and gave him my number. I didn't know that he was a series regular on the show (I didn't watch the show, and when I was on set, I spent most of my time fantasizing about what Dick looked like naked). We'd had a brief conversation once and I assumed he was another background artist. So what the hell? After hearing that I gave out my number, Dick confronted me.

"You gave *the actor* your number?"

"Why? Jealous?"

"He's a doctor on the show! You could get fired."

I don't know if I really could've gotten fired for giving a dude my number, but after learning who he was, I could certainly see how the higher-ups might worry that I was a delusional stalker. (How right they'd be—just about the wrong guy.)

I had a distorted view of courtship. I'd spent a lot of my life aggressively chasing the guys I wanted, despite having read over and over again that men loved chasing women. I couldn't help it. I still can't help it. When I want something, I go for it. I'm too worried that I'll regret it if I don't. But aggressiveness, especially when it's coming from a woman who wants to rip your pants off, can be intimidating. I've been told by more than one friend that they would describe me as "aggro." It makes me a great businesswoman but not a great romantic partner. I go at warp speed, in my head *and* in real life.

No matter how delusional I may have been, Dick eventually said I was growing on him. I'd spend the night at his house, we'd text while we both worked, and he'd confide in me. He told me his brother had committed suicide. Just like my sister. It seemed like more than a coincidence— I took it as a sign that we belonged together.

Dick and I dated for two years and some change, but the only consistent thing about our relationship was that he would cheat on me every three months. And every three months he would admit his infidelity, cry, and say he was sorry. He blamed his behavior on his brother's suicide, saying it had left him broken and damaged. Convinced that this was just a test of our love, I told myself that I understood the whole self-sabotage thing. I'd been there. After all, I'd run away from doing stand-up for the same reasons, hadn't I? Wasn't that what guilt made you do— ruin the good thing in your life?

Though Dick was a serial cheater, we had good times. We laughed very hard together, had our own weird games, and talked about everything and anything (mostly death, for obvious reasons). He could be very generous and very kind. He cried about his brother a lot, and I comforted him. I even wrote him songs, which I would only play for him if he closed his eyes because I was insecure. I was so infatuated with this guy that I agreed to have an open relationship when he insisted on it.

And I hated it. I had sex with one other man (with Dick's encouragement, ew) and it felt emotionally confusing. I'm not cut out for casual sex. I can't be intimate with someone unless I have romantic feelings (or delusions) for them.

Instead of walking away from him and the clearly toxic relationship, I became one of those paranoid snoops, going through all of his shit when he left the house. I found out his phone's passcode and would wait until he fell asleep to pore over his messages. They were never good. Girls were always sending him dirty photos, which would lead me to scream and wake him up. Then he'd get mad that I'd violated his privacy, and the cycle would repeat.

I realized he was a sex addict when I hacked into his computer and saw that he'd been trolling chubby-chaser sites. He had a string of emails with women of all shapes and sizes. Up until this point, I'd wondered why I wasn't pretty enough or smart enough to hold his attention. Why did he need other women? But now it finally all made sense. It's not that I wasn't enough. No one was enough for him. He had an insatiable urge.

Despite these very clear red flags, we stayed together

for two and a half years . . . during which time I got pregnant.

I wasn't great at taking the pill. I was working four jobs, attending comedy and acting classes, and filming videos every week. I'd go to sleep late and wake up early, often forgetting to take a pill that day because I was running late for my morning gig. But whatever, right? I wasn't going to get *pregnant*. I'd already lost my sister; surely the universe would give me a break.

One morning I was taking a shower and my nipples felt *weird*. I knew instantly. I went to the drugstore, awkwardly paid for my single item while avoiding eye contact with the cashier, and peed in their bathroom three times. The results confirmed what I already knew: smiley face, smiley face, smiley fucking face.

The conversation (if you could call it that) that Dick and I had was short: he told me his sister had had an abortion years ago, and now she was an adult and ready for the baby she had on the way! The same could be said for me! This wasn't a great time for me to have kids—I should wait until I was older, much older, and probably with another guy, to have a baby!

Seriously. He told me I would probably have a baby with another guy.

But there was no real discussion about what we would do. To him, there was only one option: abort. I wasn't so sure. I wanted to think it through. After all, I had spent years secretly judging my friends for getting abortions.

How could they *destroy* a life like that? A life that was half their own? How could they refuse adoption? I thought of them as selfish human beings who killed something that never stood a chance. The view was great from that high-ass horse.

But of course, when it happens to you, you go through the same reality check that they do.

Am I ready to be a mom? No.

Does Dick want to be a dad? No.

Do I have the financial means to support a child? No. I can barely afford to feed my three cats.

Would I give up my cats to support this kid? No.

Would I give up my *career* for a kid neither of us wanted? No.

If I had a kid, I would resent him/her for getting in the way of my dreams. Dick wouldn't have married me, so I'd probably be a single mom, still clinging to the idea that two broken people could complete each other. I eventually came to the same conclusion as Dick: neither of us was fit to be a parent. I could almost see him mentally fist-bumping himself.

We went to Planned Parenthood. Dick stayed in the waiting room while I went to see the doctor. They told me I was only seven days pregnant—the doctor was very impressed when I told him my clairvoyant nipple story— and I was given an abortion pill. I was told I'd have to stay at home all day resting, as I'd bleed heavily and experience excruciating cramps for the next few hours. I thanked them, took the pill, and left. Dick wasn't in the waiting room. He didn't respond to my calls. So while I waited for him (he was my ride home), I went to a store to get something to eat.

What the doctor didn't tell me about the pill is that it makes you nauseous. I threw up in the trash bin inside the store. Everyone looked at me in disgust and horror, and because I was so embarrassed, I blurted out, "I'm sorry! I'm pregnant!"

If I'm being honest, I loved the shift that occurred right then. Everyone's revolted expressions immediately morphed into ones of sympathy. The clerk behind the counter rushed to get me some water, gently patting me on the back. Girls looked on with what seemed like admiration in their eyes—oh, pregnancy, that must mean someone wants her, that must mean she is loved.

And while I'm being honest, I'll admit that I *liked* being thought of as pregnant. It made me want to walk around with a pregnant belly and see how I would be treated. All the doors that would be opened for me! Perhaps people would even offer to buy me something to eat. For some reason, I see a lot of pregnant women being offered food. #Dreams.

I imagined being nine months pregnant. I imagined raising a child. I imagined a completely different path for myself. But there was one thing I wanted in order to go down that path: someone who truly loved me. Someone who would be with me every step of the way. Someone who I could trust to be there when I walked out of Planned Parenthood.

At that moment I knew I wanted to be a mom but that this wasn't my time to be one. I knew that if I brought a child into the world, I wanted to give him or her the best chance. I wanted to be in a position to give a child all of my love and attention. I wanted to be with a man who loved me, in a relationship where a child was wanted.

Dick finally showed up and took me home. I bled and cried and cramped for three hours, with a hot water bottle on my stomach and Netflix documentaries playing on the TV. He took care of me as best he could, which means that he was texting a lot and occasionally checking in. There wasn't much he could do, but he definitely didn't meet my cuddle expectations.

I lay there, wondering about the life I was getting rid of. Would it have been a boy or a girl? What would he or she have been like? Maybe this was the baby who'd have grown into the person who cured cancer. Or maybe it would have grown up to be a mass shooter and I was preventing a tragedy. So many what-if scenarios played out in my mind. I wondered if I was doing the right thing. If this was murder. If I was a bad person. If I'd ever have children again.

But I was done with being delusional. I knew the kindest thing I could do was to not have the baby. It deserved to have the same childhood I'd had: two loving parents who were ready to raise a family together. I cried, thinking about how badly I wanted that someday. I wondered if I would ever have it. I worried that something would go horribly wrong with this abortion pill and I'd be left barren because of it.

When it was over, I touched my stomach and vowed that I would never go through that shit again. The next time I got pregnant, it would be when I was ready.

And I haven't been pregnant since. Cue the parade.

If I'm *ever* concerned that there may be a chance, I buy Plan B—the morning-after pill. I've mentally apologized to all the high school friends I judged when they confided in me that they'd gotten abortions. And secretly, to this day, I still wonder how psychic my nipples are. That's insane, right? How did they know? I felt like Karen from *Mean Girls*: there's a 70 percent chance you're already pregnant.

After the abortion was over, Dick took my hand. He stroked my head, looked into my eyes, and asked, "So, how would you like to pay me back for your half of the abortion? We could do $10 a week, or . . . ?"

I wish that I could say that Dick and I broke up after this.

But we didn't.

I still thought Dick was my spiritual soulmate. That he was the only person who could possibly understand what I had been through, and vice versa. He was tall and handsome. I liked the way he smelled and the color of his eyes and that he took me to Buddhist meditation sessions. He made me push past my boundaries, both physically and mentally.

He's the reason I went on a seven-day silent meditation retreat. Funnily enough, he bailed on that retreat at the last minute. And even funnier, the retreat is the thing that gave me the strength to finally leave him. A few days after I'd gotten back, he showed up at my house in the morning, crying. He'd cheated again.

While I'd been off for a week in a secluded temple in Joshua Tree, my days spent alternating between half-hour sessions of silent walking and sitting meditation, he'd found someone at a bar and hooked up with them. I'd just spent seven grueling days in complete silence (except for the two times I caved and called Dick just for the reassurance that sound still existed). I had spent seven days sitting with myself, walking with myself, and living with myself.

On the last day of my retreat, a day when we could finally talk to one another, I felt like I'd found myself. We all had to go around and say one word that summed up our experience. People said words like "love" and "whole" and "discovery." I was the last one to go. I said the famous word from Mary Poppins: "supercalifragilisticexpialidocious."

Everyone laughed.

And it clicked: *this is me.*

I'm a person who makes other people laugh. It was one of the only moments in my life when I've been 100 percent sure of who I am. I felt truly peaceful and I loved myself without shame or neurosis or arrogance.

While I was having the most revealing, vulnerable, and

self-loving moment of my life, Dick was sticking his dick in someone else.

So when he showed up at my door, crying and begging for forgiveness in the early hours of the morning, I finally thought: fuck this guy. I didn't hate him, but after spending seven silent days with myself in the desert, I had finally found my self-esteem. I knew I deserved better than this. I wanted someone who wouldn't cheat on me every three months. Someone who loved himself enough to love me. Someone who didn't try to come up with a payment plan for an abortion the moment after it happened. I gave Dick a hug and I told him it was over between us. Out in the desert, I'd finally found some self-respect.

So . . . have you taken your birth control today?

The Hardest Part of Being in an Emotionally Abusive Relationship Is Actually Admitting That You're in One

---

Right after my breakup with Dick, I wanted to focus on myself. I had just come from a beautiful experience in the desert, and I wanted to take full advantage of the wisdom that I'd found there. I vowed to stay single and spend more time alone.

Then I met Cameron.

Cameron had the kind of confidence that only comes from self-made success. He was funny and handsome and he knew it. He was sharp and direct, and we were immediately attracted to each other.

We dated hard and fast, moving in together after three months. The first six months of our relationship were wonderful. We were having sex every single day, frequently going out on dates, and falling deeply in love with each other. Cameron was intelligent and thoughtful and could make me laugh. I admired him. He felt too good to be true.

And he was. Our fights would often end with him storming out of our apartment. I'd call him and he'd turn off his phone, so I'd cry until he decided to call me back or return home. Once the honeymoon phase was over, he became distant. He devoted himself to work, and it was all he wanted to do or talk about. He became increasingly frustrated with his business and colleagues, often citing them as the reason for ruining our night.

I had my first panic attack with him. We were sitting in a restaurant when all of a sudden I started hyperventilating. I had no idea what was happening to me. I felt afraid for no reason, I was short of breath, and my heart started pounding. He didn't know what to do, and I couldn't communicate what I needed from him. He asked for the bill so that we could leave, but I told him not to. He was confused: Did I want to leave or not? I didn't know. I felt frozen—and all I wanted to do was wait for it to be over. I told him no, I didn't want to leave just yet, but he paid the bill anyway.

We left the restaurant, but he was furious that I couldn't communicate. He said he had no idea what I wanted and why I was being so difficult. He started screaming at me and said I was a bitch. I was surprised by his behavior. He was someone who'd suffered from panic attacks before. When we'd be out socializing, he'd sometimes have the exact same symptoms and I'd gently lead us out of the venue until he calmed down. Instead of recognizing what I was going through as something he knew all too well, he assumed I was being difficult.

I walked on eggshells around him. I'd be singing in the kitchen and all of a sudden I'd hear this terrifyingly raw scream. I'd run over to the bathroom, thinking he must have fallen and broken something, and ask what was wrong and if he was okay. And through the bathroom door he'd tell me to *shut the fuck up,* to stop singing because I was pissing him the fuck off.

My response, of course, was to cry. He would apologize. I'd forgive him and dismiss the yelling as a by-product of stress or hunger. Then we'd make up until something else I did pissed him off.

Friends and family tried to warn me. A friend of mine said, "You're like a light. And he's this anchor, weighing you down." I called her dramatic, and jokingly told Cameron. He was furious. He didn't want me to hang out with her anymore. I agreed; if she didn't support my relationship, why should I support our friendship?

My family wasn't very fond of him either. He rarely came to any family functions I invited him to, and when he did come, he was sullen and quiet. My family's attempts at conversation were met with short, one-word replies. At one point he even told me, "I don't give a fuck about your friends or family." He's just cranky, I told myself. He doesn't mean it.

The last fight we ever had occurred when I was trying to do his bookkeeping for him. I'd noticed that he hadn't been paid for some work he'd done months earlier. When I tried to explain this to him, he exploded. "YOU HAVE NO FUCKING IDEA WHAT YOU'RE TALKING ABOUT, DO YOU?!" he shouted.

I was more taken aback than hurt. "What?" I asked, stunned. "I'm trying to tell you that—"

"I DON'T WANT TO TALK ABOUT THIS ANY-MORE!"

That was the moment it clicked for me. I was telling him I'd found him money, and he was *screaming* at me. This man would never treat me with respect. He'd never stop screaming at me.

Was this how I wanted my relationship to be?

My future marriage?

No. Who the hell wants that?

It was over.

It took me a year of therapy to finally accept that I was in an emotionally abusive relationship. There was a part of me that would always think, "But he's never hit me. So it's not abuse. Right?" I didn't see the manipulation, jealousy, domination, and constant blame as abuse. I didn't see the bursts of anger, screaming, put-downs, and shaming as abuse. I'd make excuses for his unacceptable behavior, rationalizing it in my head. I'd shrugged off the label in therapy sessions before, saying I didn't *feel* abused. Was he a bad boyfriend sometimes? Sure. An abuser? That felt too . . . dramatic, I guess. It felt weird. I didn't want to acknowledge it. Didn't want to own that label.

But my feelings didn't change the facts. I was in an abusive relationship. Every success I had was met with jealousy. Instead of congratulating me when I signed with a new management company, he told me I was lucky. Then he sulked for the rest of the day. When there was an article written about one of my short films, he said, "It must have been a slow news day." He would always claim he was joking, but I knew him well enough at that point. He wasn't. Any success I had threatened his own.

If he was talking and I said something in response, I was *interrupting*. He would close his mouth and shake his head, furious that I'd interrupted him, refusing to talk further. We often argued about that. What's a conversation if I'm not responding? I'd ask. It's a monologue, that's what. That only pissed him off further.

He shamed me for past relationships or decisions. He'd control my friendships, telling me which friends he approved of and which ones he no longer wanted me to see. He'd belittle my accomplishments and projects. He was always right and I was always wrong.

Over the course of our two-and-a-half-year relationship, he isolated me from my friends and family. I couldn't imagine a life where we weren't together because he was all I had. I was so deeply entrenched that I felt like I was going crazy.

I'm not an innocent victim in all this. I was a willing participant in this relationship. And I wasn't perfect. I'd often lie and tell him what I thought he wanted to hear. (I was afraid of his anger, but that's not an excuse.) I'm sure when he tells the story of our relationship, he has a very different perspective on it. I doubt he ever meant to be malicious. Maybe he just wanted a trophy wife, someone to stand behind him instead of beside him. But that's not me.

I recently talked to a friend who just got out of an emotionally abusive relationship. She told me that at one point she'd tried to break up with her boyfriend, and he raped her. I was speechless. She nodded slowly and said it had taken her a long time to be able to say that. It's taken her a very long time to accept the label of what happened to her. She had always thought of rape as "a stranger attacks you in a dark alley and you scream but no one can hear you." She never thought it would be her boyfriend, forcing himself on her as her body shut down and her mind went elsewhere to protect itself.

She said that even after that incident, she was hesitant to call the relationship abusive. I understood. When you're in the trenches, you become detached from reality. You don't know what's right or wrong. You've been told "you're crazy, you're overreacting" so many times, you start to believe that's the truth.

If you think you may be in an abusive relationship, get some distance and seek support from a therapist or your friends. The sooner you can clear your head, the better you can judge whether or not your relationship is toxic, codependent, abusive, or something else.

After I'd had enough time away from Cameron, I recognized when I analyzed his actions with my therapist that I'd been in a verbally/emotionally abusive relationship. He was constantly yelling at me, whether it was a demand (shut the fuck up) or an insult (you don't know what you're fucking talking about) or to cuss at me (see previous two). He made fun of me, insulted my ideas, made negative comments about people I loved, dismissed as jokes remarks that offended me, treated me like a child, was emotionally unavailable, and would disengage whenever it suited him. And to top it all off, his favorite pet name for me was "faggot."

I was nervous when I approached him about certain topics, felt the need to tell him about innocent events in case he heard about them through other people and accused me of lying, and felt misunderstood for most of our relationship. He made me doubt my sanity and my intelligence.

I stayed for as long as I did because I hoped he would change. I wanted us to go back to the honeymoon phase. I was holding on to the hope that the guy I'd first met would return. But without long-term therapy and a willingness to change, abusive relationships don't get better. Partners who yell and cuss at you won't suddenly stop. The jealousy, resentment, blaming, and entitlement don't magically go away. If you find yourself making excuses for hurtful behavior—he's working on a deadline, he's worried about family stuff, he just feels like everything is out of control—hit pause for a minute. If the situation were reversed, is that how *you* would deal with stress? How *you* would regain control? If you wouldn't do it, stop making those excuses.

I'll never forget one of the last things Cameron ever said to me: "You'll never be happy with a nice guy. That's not enough for you."

He couldn't have been more wrong.

Nice Guys Don't Finish Last

—

They say you can't choose who you fall in love with.

But you can.

Think about it. It may seem like you're automatically drawn to bad boys and assholes, but take a step back and you'll see how wrong that is. Everywhere you look, movies and books and TV are teaching us that more conflict means more passion. That you should completely change who you are to be in a relationship with John Travolta in *Grease*. That unless you're crying, you're not *feeling*.

I wish the advice I'd gotten when I was younger was to find a man who adores me. To find a man who will make a good dad. To find someone who radiates kindness, is reliable, and cares for others. These qualities are always going to result in a more loving, fulfilling relationship.

Last year I found myself in the healthiest relationship

of my life. My boyfriend, Brad, is a man who has no agenda. He's transparent, kind, and funny. He fights for what he believes in. He's calm but firm in times of crisis or confrontation. He's the kind of guy who would be portrayed in movies as the nice guy who just doesn't quite have chemistry with the lead, who's outshined by the other guy, the one who keeps her guessing. The one she fights like mad with.

That makes for good entertainment. But in real life? It'll make you miserable.

Sure, Brad and I fight, but there's none of the screaming and crying and storming out that I used to associate with passion. It's calm and reasonable and full of understanding. I'm not walking on eggshells around him. I can be completely honest without the fear that he'll walk out on me. It's the kind of relationship that makes me wake up and realize, "Oh. This is exactly what I want my life with someone to be like."

Several of my friends are now finding partners like this. Nice, good men who adore you. Who treat you well and are affectionate and kind. Who are understanding when you're stressed. Who are endlessly supportive. They're men who brag about your accomplishments to everyone who will listen. The kind who trust you, no matter where you are or who you're with, and vice versa.

A friend of mine recently got married. At her wedding, she credited her mom for her successful relationship: "Early on, my mother told me, 'Find a good man who will always treat you well. Even when the fireworks are gone.' "

When I was a teenager and even in my early twenties, I never thought that I would fall for someone who was so transparent. What you see is what you get with Brad, and what everyone sees is a kind soul. I grew up believing that these sensitive and attentive men were all wrong. That you should be chasing some brooding, emotional man you can't quite reach. Someone with deep pain in their past and smoldering eyes. Someone who could barely talk about their past because it was so riddled with trauma.

But I know now that it's all bullshit.

Don't look for success; it's fleeting.

Don't go for looks; those will fade. We all get old and wrinkly.

Don't look for money; that power dynamic is full of problems.

Don't fall for mystery; you don't know what he could possibly be hiding.

Find someone who will inspire you to be a better person, who will make you laugh even when you don't feel like it, and who is good to you no matter how tough things are. And strive to be that person for them.

Oh, and look for a guy who will let you have six cats even though he's allergic. That's how you know you've got a keeper.

———

Relationships have taught me so much about myself and how to be a more loving, patient, and overall better human being. No mat-

ter who my partner is or how we end, there's always something I can learn from what we went through together to incorporate into my life.

Thanks for the broken hearts, boys. Now I know how to put myself back together.

Choose Life

—

Every single moment of every single day, we are floating. We live on a floating rock, hurtling through outer space, in an endless expansion of gas balls, black holes, and other floating rocks.

My sister died. My whole family will die. I will die.

Some people may think this is morbid, but really? These are just facts. There's a freedom in accepting them. Maybe nothing matters, but that means all the bad stuff doesn't matter either. That embarrassing audition I had this morning doesn't matter. The broken friendships over the years don't matter. The only things that matter are the ones that you decide matter. It's up to you to choose what to do with the time you're given on this earth.

Whenever someone complains about how old they are, I always say that age is a privilege. Not everyone gets to grow old. Cherish it. Because who the hell knows what happens after we die? Really, *who the hell knows?* In my mind, death is the absence of consciousness. It's nothing. Not even a black abyss. Just nothing. That lack of space between falling asleep and waking up after anesthesia.

If I'm proven wrong, that'll be great. Maybe there is a heaven. Maybe I will see Kristina again. But if not, all I know is what I have now. All I can experience is however many years I have left. It's a beautiful, empowering thing to realize.

MY SISTER'S DEATH GAVE my life purpose. It's the reason I am who I am today. Death is our only guarantee, yet so many of us don't realize how real it is until we've been directly affected by it. We all know we're going to die someday, but we live as if that isn't true.

Kristina taught me the greatest lessons anyone can know. That death, though random and horrible and frightful, is nothing to be afraid of. That getting older is a privilege not everyone experiences. That there is no point in living if you're not doing what you love, if you're not surrounding yourself with people who love and inspire you.

Life isn't short; it's long. It's everything we know. It tricks us into thinking that it's going to go on forever. We are all lost, confused, and doing the best that we can with what we have. I certainly don't have all the answers, and most of the time I still feel lost. But because of Kristina, I've learned to make use of the time I've been given, to work hard at pursuing my passion, and to love fiercely and truly.

So I will end this book by saying what I said at the beginning: This book is for you, Kristina. Everything I have done, and will do, is because of you. My life is a letter to you that I will never burn.

You were an amazing person I had the honor of knowing for thirteen years. You inspire me every day. You were fearless, talented, and bold. I think of you when I walk onstage, step in front of the camera, or confront a fear. I hope that wherever you are, if you are still out there, that we get to meet again. I hope that you're proud of me.

I love you, Kristina Marie Akana. And I will never forget you.

ACKNOWLEDGMENTS

There's a handful of people I'd love to thank for helping me stay sane while writing this book: Brad Gage, for appeasing every anxious feeling I had along the way and reading the book more times than anyone ever will. Gabby, Lauren, and Jackie, for being lifelong friends and forever foodies. Tom Spriggs, for always reminding me of the bigger picture. The Coronel Group's Leanne and Mike. My wonderful team at UTA: Ali Barash, Ty Flynn, and Shauna Perlman. And Sara Weiss, my editor, who helped me shape these raw emotions into a book.

ABOUT THE AUTHOR

ANNA AKANA started her YouTube channel in 2011, jump-starting her career as an actress, producer, filmmaker, and writer. Now with over 1.7 million subscribers, Anna produces one short film a month for her channel, in addition to her weekly YouTube show, which features semi-autobiographical comedic stories where she portrays multiple roles.

As a screen actress, Akana can be seen in recurring roles on Freeform's *The Fosters* and Comedy Central's *Hampton Deville,* as well as in the films *Hello, My Name Is Doris, Ant-Man,* and the upcoming thriller *You Get Me.* She is also the creator of the clothing company Ghost & Stars. She lives in Los Angeles with her six cats.

annaakana.com
YouTube.com/user/AnnaAkana
Twitter: @AnnaAkana

ABOUT THE TYPE

This book was set in Bembo, a typeface based on
an old-style Roman face that was used for
Cardinal Pietro Bembo's tract *De Aetna* in 1495.
Bembo was cut by Francesco Griffo (1450–1518)
in the early sixteenth century for Italian
Renaissance printer and publisher
Aldus Manutius (1449–1515). The Lanston
Monotype Company of Philadelphia brought
the well-proportioned letterforms of Bembo
to the United States in the 1930s.